CA 0563 486325 9001 ✓

KT-174-502

Dun Laoghaire-Rathdown Libraries
CABINTEELY LIBRARY
Inv/05 : J398J   Price E11.78
Title: Monsters and villains
Class: J791.4572

DOCTOR · WHO

MONSTERS AND VILLAINS

BY JUSTIN RICHARDS

BAINTE DEN STOC

WITHDRAWN FROM DÚN LAOGHAIRE RATHDOWN
COUNTY LIBRARY STOCK

BAINTE DEN STOC

WITHDRAWN FROM DÚN LAOGHAIRE RATHDOWN
COUNTY LIBRARY STOCK

BBC
BOOKS

Published by BBC Books, BBC Worldwide Ltd, Woodlands, 80 Wood Lane, London W12 0TT

First published 2005. Reprinted 2005

Copyright © Justin Richards 2005, except: extracts from original television scripts and writers' quotes all copyright © their respective authors. Additional material copyright © Russell T Davies, 2005. The moral right of the author has been asserted.
Doctor Who logo © BBC 2004. Tardis image © BBC 1963. Dalek image © BBC/Terry Nation 1963. Licensed by BBC Worldwide Limited.

Original series broadcast on BBC television. Format © BBC 1963.
'Doctor Who', 'TARDIS' and 'DALEK' and the Doctor Who logo are trademarks of the British Broadcasting Corporation and are used under licence.

All rights reserved. No part of this book may be reproduced in any form or by any means without prior written permission from the publisher, except by a reviewer, who may quote brief passages in a review.

ISBN 0563 48632 5

Commissioning Editors:	Shirley Patton and Stuart Cooper
Project Editor:	Vicki Vrint
Creative Director:	Justin Richards
Design:	Lee Binding
Cover Design:	Lee Binding
Production Controller:	Peter Hunt

Doctor Who is a BBC Wales production for BBC ONE. Executive Producers: Russell T Davies, Julie Gardner and Mal Young.
Producer: Phil Collinson.

Printed in Great Britain by CPI Bath. Colour Origination by Butler & Tanner Ltd.

BBC Books would like to thank the following for providing photographs and for permission to reproduce copyright material. While every effort has been made to trace and acknowledge all copyright holders, we would like to apologise should there have been any errors or omissions.
All images copyright © BBC, except:
page 27 (bottom left, bottom middle, bottom right) Raymond P. Cusick
page 28 (bottom middle) the Hulton Picture Library
page 31 (bottom right) the Topham Picture Source
page 35 (middle) Andrew Beech
page 40 (bottom left, bottom middle) David Richardson
page 41 (illustrations) Raymond P. Cusick
page 43 (all images) Mike Tucker
page 47 (bottom right) Miss Susan Moore
page 92 (top, middle) Tony Cornell

BAINTE DEN STOC

WITHDRAWN FROM DÚN LAOGHAIRE RATHDOWN COUNTY LIBRARY STOCK

Leabharlanna Dhún Laoghaire - Ráth An Dúin

With additional thanks to:

Stephen Cole	David J. Howe
Russell T Davies	Gwenllian Llwyd
Ben Dunn	Helen Raynor
Sarah Emsley	Elwen Rowland
Jacqueline Farrow	Matthew Savage
Cameron Fitch	Robert Shearman
Mark Gatiss	Edward Thomas
Ian Grutchfield	Mike Tucker
Clayton Hickman	

CONTENTS

MONSTERS AND VILLAINS

The first episode of **Doctor Who** was shown on 23 November 1963. The programme then ran on BBC ONE every year up until 1989. Now it is back – and as the saying goes 'it's about time'. In that very first episode, the Doctor was an enigma, a mystery. Just as viewers new to the series today wonder who he could be and what is inside that Police Box he calls his TARDIS, so they did back then. But from the second-ever story, it was clear what the Doctor did – he fought the monsters. That second story was called *The Daleks* and it introduced a creature that would become almost as popular as the Doctor himself. The Daleks have changed little since 1963. But, ironically, the Doctor has changed.

To keep the show running, it was necessary to replace the original actor, William Hartnell. He played the Doctor as a grumpy old man who, over time, came to respect his human companions. It was a shock to them – and to the audience – when the Doctor collapsed to the floor of the TARDIS and changed. He became a new Doctor, with a very different character, as respected actor Patrick Troughton took over the role.

Three years later, Jon Pertwee became the new Doctor, and we discovered that the Doctor was a Time Lord, one of a race of incredibly long-lived people who have the ability to 'regenerate' whenever a body wears out. Tom Baker, Peter Davison, Colin Baker and Sylvester McCoy played the Doctor in the years that followed, and Paul McGann starred in the 1996 TV movie version of **Doctor Who**.

Now the Doctor is played by Christopher Eccleston, and he is still a mysterious alien who travels through time and space, and stands against the monsters, just as he always has. Because there are always monsters. There have been monsters for as long as there have been stories. And there have always been villains. Combine the two, create a terrible monster that is also a ruthless, evil villain and surely you can't go wrong.

With the new series, the monsters and villains have started off right where they belong – as the very essence of the stories. In this book we look at just some of those the Doctor has defeated in the past and that he and Rose battle against today, as well as more friendly alien creatures. We explore how these aliens came into being – how the writers imagined them, and how the designers created them. Here you can see how the original scripts changed – as all scripts do – for the actual production. You can compare initial concept drawings with the final creatures. And you can rest assured that there are plenty more monsters and villains waiting for the Doctor and Rose in the past, present and future.

A new Doctor faces a new monster – the Slitheen.

While they are not named explicitly in the episode *Rose*, the shop dummies that come to life and that menace the Doctor and Rose are called Autons. First encountered by the Doctor in his third incarnation, the creatures are blank-faced, plastic humanoids created by the Nestene Consciousness and animated by a tiny portion of its collective being. Each Auton has a gun hidden inside its hand, the fingers dropping away to allow it to fire. Bullets have no effect on the Autons.

THE NESTENE CONSCIOUSNESS

The Doctor describes the Nestene Consciousness as 'a ruthlessly aggressive intelligent alien life form'. It is, literally, living plastic – able to take on any shape. Since the so-called Time War when its food-stock planets were destroyed, it has mutated from a disembodied, mutually telepathic intelligence into a living plastic desperate to find further food stocks from which to renew itself.

Faces of shop window Autons depend on style of other 'real' mannequins

Auton is made entirely from plastic, and is impervious to bullets

Hand gun – fingers drop away to reveal deadly weapon

Each Auton is animated and controlled by a portion of the Nestene Consciousness

A new Doctor and his assistant, Liz Shaw, face the Autons for the very first time.

SPEARHEAD FROM SPACE

Written by
Robert Holmes
Featuring
the Third Doctor,
UNIT and Liz
First broadcast
3 January 1970 –
24 January 1970
4 episodes

The TARDIS lands in the middle of a strange meteorite shower, and the Doctor swiftly discovers the Nestene plan to colonise Earth. Killer Autons are collecting the 'meteorites' that contain fragments of the Nestene Consciousness. At the nearby Auto Plastics factory, the Nestene Consciousness creates killer Autons and facsimiles of people.

The recovering Doctor works with his old friend Brigadier Lethbridge-Stewart, who is in charge of UNIT, to stop the invasion. Together with Doctor Elizabeth Shaw, he creates a weapon to stop the invaders. But with shop-window dummies and Madame Tussauds waxworks coming to life he may already be too late.

EXILED TO EARTH

After many years of wandering through space and time in the TARDIS, the Doctor was captured by his own people, the Time Lords, and put on trial for interfering in the affairs of other planets. He put up a spirited defence, accusing the Time Lords of complacency and inaction, but nevertheless he was found guilty and sentenced to exile – with a new appearance – on Earth in the late twentieth century.

Earth was chosen as it has always been a favourite planet of the Doctor and seemed vulnerable to attack.

UNIT

After Colonel Lethbridge-Stewart's involvement in foiling the plans of the Great Intelligence (see page 91) the United Nations set up its own Intelligence Taskforce – UNIT – to deal with such otherworldly threats. With a remit to investigate the unusual and the alien, UNIT's first major battle was against the Cybermen (see page 19). With the arrival of the exiled Doctor to act as Scientific Advisor to the British contingent of UNIT, headed by Brigadier Lethbridge-Stewart, the organisation was immediately pitched against the Nestene threat.

COLONISATION

The Nestene Consciousness is a living plastic, able to create forms for itself on any planet it wishes to colonise – forms ideally suited to conquest. It has been colonising worlds for a thousand million years.

The real General Scobie (the Brigadier's superior) is exhibited in Madame Tussauds while his plastic double takes over.

THE ENERGY UNITS

The energy units are rough spheres about thirty centimetres in diameter, each containing a fraction of the Nestene Consciousness. They glow with the Nestene power and are made of a form of plastic.

The units are sent to Earth through a funnel of super-heated air, landing like meteorites, and are then collected by the Autons. After their first attempted invasion, one unit was left intact. But it was subsequently stolen by the Master, and the energy inside used to create more Autons in preparation for a second attempted invasion.

CHANNING

Until the recovery of the Swarm Leader, Channing forms the spearhead of the first invasion attempt. He controls Hibbert, managing director of Auto Plastics, and directs the Autons.

Since they are all essentially part of the same being, Channing can see what any of the Autons or facsimiles sees and can direct them mentally.

KILLER AUTONS

With their crudely formed faces and bland overalls, the Autons are not designed to blend in with human society. Their function is to collect the energy units and protect the spearhead of the invasion. The name Auton is derived from Auto Plastics – the factory where the first Autons were made.

The shop-window dummies used in two of the attempted invasions (above) are essentially killer Autons. Their function is to create havoc and destroy, so the Nestenes can take over.

FACSIMILES

The Nestene Consciousness can create perfect plastic copies of politicians and others in strategic positions. During its first attempted invasion, these facsimiles were stored in a display at Madame Tussauds waxworks until activated and sent to take the places of the original people. The exception was General Scobie, who was activated early to hamper UNIT investigations.

In its third attempted invasion, it copies Rose's boyfriend, Mickey, to track down the Doctor through Rose and discover how much he knows.

With the Autons defeated, the Master appears to surrender to UNIT.

TERROR OF THE AUTONS

Written by
Robert Holmes
Featuring
the Third Doctor,
UNIT and Jo
First broadcast
2 January 1971 –
23 January 1971
4 episodes

The Time Lords warn the Doctor that an old enemy of his – the Master – has come to Earth. The Master reactivates an energy unit and creates more Autons. He plans to aid the Nestene Consciousness in another attempt to invade Earth, promising to help it establish a bridgehead and create panic using deadly plastic daffodils.

As UNIT battle against killer Autons disguised in grotesque carnival masks for a supposed plastics promotional tour, the Doctor persuades the Master that the Nestene Consciousness will not honour its agreement with him. Together the two Time Lords manage to send the creature back into deep space.

FAKE POLICE

Investigating the circus where the Master has hidden his TARDIS (disguised as a horse box), the Doctor and Jo are attacked by an angry mob. They are saved by two policemen. But in fact the policemen are Autons, as the Doctor realises. He rips the face mask from one of them and, with the help of UNIT, the Doctor and Jo escape. During the battle, Captain Yates drives a car straight at one Auton and knocks it over a cliff. When it tumbles to the bottom, it simply gets to its feet and starts to climb back up.

DEADLY DAFFODILS

The killer daffodils – or Nestene Autojets, as the Master calls them – have their instructions imprinted on every cell as a program-pattern, which reveals a nose and mouth when converted to 'visual symbols'. Activated by radio signal, the daffodils spray plastic film over the nose and mouth of their victim. This film is then dissolved by the carbon dioxide from the lungs as the victim dies. The Master plans to set off the daffodils with a radio impulse. The Autons have distributed almost half a million daffodils – each designed to kill.

Shop dummies come to life in the basement of a department store.

LIVING PLASTIC

The alien Nestene Consciousness can bring anything made of plastic to life. It can use thought control to activate plastic to act as its eyes and ears, as well as animate it – often with deadly results. It is only when plastic starts to come to life that we realise how much we rely on and use the material.

KILLER CABLE

Having failed to kill the Doctor with a booby-trap bomb and the killer Autons, the Master resorts to a more subtle approach. Disguised as a telephone engineer, he gets into UNIT HQ and replaces the flex on the Doctor's telephone with a longer, plastic cord. He then calls the Doctor and transmits an activation signal down the phone.

Imbued with Nestene intelligence, the phone cable comes to life and attempts to throttle the Doctor, who is only saved by the timely intervention of the Brigadier.

LIVING DOLL

To kill Mr Farrell, owner of the plastics factory he is using to create Autons and daffodils, the Master uses a grotesque, troll-like doll. Activated by heat, the doll comes to life and kills Farrell. Trying to discover its secrets, the Doctor finds out that the doll is made from solid plastic. It again comes to life and attacks Jo when Captain Yates is using the Doctor's Bunsen burner to make cocoa. It is destroyed when Yates shoots it to bits.

FIENDISH FURNITURE

When McDermott, production manager at the plastics factory, takes issue with the Master, the Master invites him to try out one of the 'new products' – a black plastic armchair. As soon as McDermott sits down, the chair folds in on itself, trapping McDermott inside and suffocating him.

THE AUTONS

Killer Autons rampage through a shopping centre.

ROSE

Written by
Russell T Davies
Featuring
the Ninth Doctor
and Rose
First broadcast
26 March 2005
1 episode

Working in a department store, Rose Tyler is attacked by shop-window dummies in the basement. She is saved by the mysterious Doctor, who tells her he is an alien stopping the attempted invasion of Earth by the Nestene Consciousness and its killer Autons.

Initially sceptical, Rose tries to find out more about the Doctor, but her enquiries lead herself and her boyfriend, Mickey, into deadly danger. Eventually, Rose helps the Doctor to find the lair of the Nestene Consciousness. Together, they manage to destroy the creature, and Rose leaves with the Doctor in his TARDIS.

ROSE

Nineteen-year-old Rose Tyler lives with her mum, Jackie, on the Powell Estate in London. She works in a large department store, where the Nestene Consciousness has concealed killer Autons among the shop-window dummies ready for an invasion. Here she meets the Doctor for the first time, and finds herself caught up in his extraordinary adventures.

THE NESTENE PLAN

The Nestene Consciousness has had its food stocks destroyed in the great Time War, which caused so much damage. Its protein planets have rotted away. So by the time of this third attempted invasion, it sees Earth as a suitable alternative food supply, made attractive by the oil, smoke, toxins and dioxins in the air. It plans to take over the world, activating Autons concealed in shops with a transmission boosted through the London Eye.

SHOP DUMMIES

To spearhead their attack on Earth, the Nestene Consciousness once again uses shop-window dummies that come to life and smash their way out of the shops to attack. As well as 'standard' killer Autons, as used in their first attempted invasion, the Nestene also creates 'child' mannequins. The Autons 'model' all manner of designer clothes – even bridal gowns.

RESURRECTING THE AUTONS

The new-look Autons for the 2005 series of **Doctor Who** were designed by Neill Gorton and Matthew Savage, under the supervision of the production designer, Edward Thomas. The original concept design is shown here.

Writer and executive producer, Russell T Davies, explains: 'I decided to bring back the Autons – although this time, the Doctor never actually uses their name! – because it was important that Rose, in her first adventure, could consider the whole thing to be one big trick. If, in the first five minutes of the episode, she saw a great big tentacled thing, then we don't have too many of those on Planet Earth – she'd know they were aliens! But plastic, even if it's living plastic, can keep her doubting for a long time, while she gets to know the Doctor. Is it radio control? Or clever prosthetics? Smoke and mirrors?

'It was an honour to resurrect the creations of one of the programme's finest writers, the late Robert Holmes – what a genius! If a small spark of his wonderful mind can touch the new series, then we're very lucky indeed. As a writer, I'd like to think this episode is a tribute to him, with love and gratitude.'

GETTING A CONSCIENCE

In *Spearhead from Space* (right), the tentacles that emerge from the tank containing the Nestene Consciousness were 'physical props' – real tentacles provided by the Visual Effects team. A model of the Consciousness was made and filmed for *Terror of the Autons*. But the final effect was not considered convincing enough, so an electronic glow was substituted. For *Rose*, the Nestene Consciousness was created as a computer-generated image (CGI), added to the film in post-production.

Left and above: The Doctor confronts the Nestene Consciousness, which prepares to attack.

THE AUTONS

AUTON ATTACK

The Autons' return gave the new production team the opportunity to enhance one small part of **Doctor Who**'s golden past. In the first Auton serial, *Spearhead from Space*, the shop-window dummies come alive in the shop windows.

As writer and executive producer Russell T Davies points out: 'The Autons step forward, they raise their arms, they slice down – and then we see nothing, the picture cuts away, and the audience hears the distant sound of glass smashing. Breakable glass panes were probably too expensive for that wonderful, inventive production team! At last, 35 years later, thanks to the brilliant technicians of BBC Wales, the audience can finally see that glass break. It was worth the wait!'

SCRIPT EXTRACTS - *ROSE*

```
JACKIE looks round.
DUMMIES are stepping down from every window. All sorts of
different shapes and sizes. And it's all strangely calm,
SHOPPERS just looking, bemused. Jackie turns to see -
THREE CHILD DUMMIES walk out of the doors of Daisy and Tom-
type shop. Faces just ovals, no features at all.
CUT TO the far end of the street. CAROLINE's scared, CLIVE
steps forward. A DUMMY turns to face him. Enraptured:

CLIVE
It's true. Everything I've read. All those stories. It's all
true.

The dummy lifts up its arm to point at him.
The wrist is hinged, its hand swings down. Revealing a metal
tube.
And Clive's so sad, because he knows what happens next:
The dummy fires.
```

Top: The Autons emerge.

Above: Jackie is caught in the mayhem.

Right: Autons on the streets of London.

Above: Deadly Autons move into action.

Right: London in the aftermath.

Far right: Caroline and her son try to escape.

JACKIE stands frozen. The world has gone
insane:
DUMMIES firing.
SHOPPERS running, screaming. (NB, see the
shots fired, but not the actual impact,
cut around that.)
A MAN has a CHILD DUMMY clinging to his
back.
CAROLINE and SON run past, screaming.
At the far end, a car is burning. Sirens
wail.
A phalanx of DUMMIES walks down the
street. Calm, elegant.
JACKIE's crying. Heaving for breath.
She's tucked away to one side, backing
away from the madness...
Behind her: a bridal shop.
Jackie's staring out, not seeing the
THREE BRIDE DUMMIES in different white
dresses step forward, raise arms, swipe
- glass shatters, CU Jackie, turning
round, screaming -

THE CYBERMEN

The Cybermen were once humans, but tried to combat their race's shortening life span with cybernetic surgery – replacing their bodily organs and limbs with mechanical versions. They also 'enhanced' their brains, removing the weakness of emotion. The result was the Cybermen – strong and efficient, not needing to breathe, but without fear or emotion, or humanity.

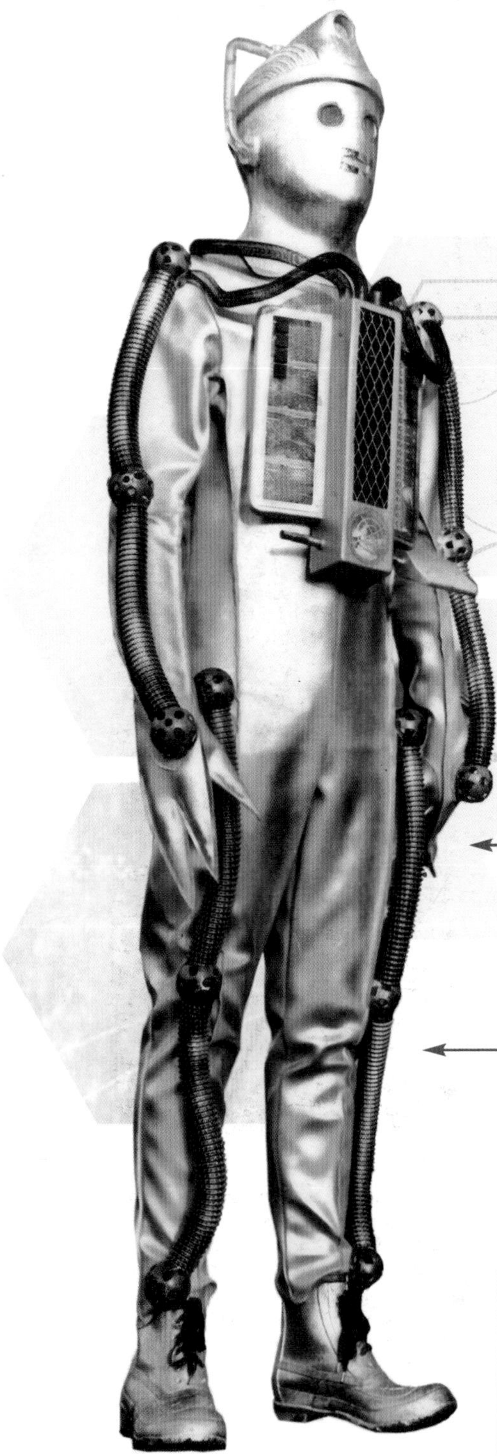

Cyberleaders are designated by black trim

Residual organic components visible

Cybermen do not need to breathe but can be 'suffocated' by gold dust

Chest unit replaces heart and lungs. Susceptible to attack by solvents

Powerful Cyberweapon

Hands evolved into three-fingered claw

Pipes for Cyberfluids integrated into Cybersuit

Tubes carry vital fluids

Soles of boots designed to grip on all surfaces

A DYING RACE

The Cybermen seem to be a race in decline. Even having extended their lives through the use of metal and plastic cybernetics, they need the resources of other worlds – especially Earth. This may be because of their affinity with human beings. The original Cybermen came from Earth's 'twin' planet Mondas, which drifted away from the solar system. Later the Cybermen adopted another planet, Telos, where they put themselves into suspended animation, frozen within huge tombs. The overriding ambition of the Cybermen is to survive.

The Cybermen approach Snowcap Base through an Antarctic blizzard.

THE TENTH PLANET

The Doctor, Polly and Ben arrive at Snowcap Base in the Antarctic, in 1986, as it monitors a space probe. A new planet enters the solar system, drawing power first from the space probe – resulting in its destruction – then from Earth itself. Cybermen arrive at Snowcap, intent on using a Z Bomb installed there to destroy the Earth before their own planet – Earth's twin, Mondas – absorbs too much energy.

With Cybermen arriving on Earth in force, the Doctor close to collapse and Polly a prisoner, it is up to Ben to fight back. He discovers the Cybermen are susceptible to radiation and manages to hold them off for long enough for Mondas to explode.

Written by
Kit Pedler
Featuring
the First Doctor,
Ben and Polly
First broadcast
8 October 1966 –
29 October 1966
4 episodes

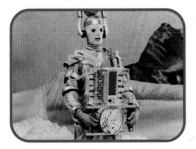

CYBER DATA

These first Cybermen have human hands, and perhaps the remains of their faces survive beneath the material that covers them. They plan to take humans back to Mondas and convert them into Cybermen like themselves. When the Cybermen speak, the mouth opens and an electronic, altered voice comes out.

But the Cybermen are susceptible to radiation, and they also draw the power that keeps them alive from their home planet. When Mondas explodes, the human material of the Cybermen 'dissolves', leaving a shrivelled husk.

CYBER NAMES

The scripts for *The Tenth Planet* (and also in places for *The Moonbase*) gave the individual Cybermen names. These were not stressed within the story, but for *The Tenth Planet* they were retained in the cast listings.

The names of the Cybermen given in the scripts for *The Tenth Planet* were: Krail, Talon, Shav, Krang, Jarl and Gern.

MONDAS

Mondas was an ancient name for Earth. The Cybermen describe their home as Earth's 'twin', and explain that aeons ago Mondas drifted away from Earth on a journey to the edge of space. Now it has returned... But the energy of Mondas is nearly exhausted and the Cybermen have brought Mondas back to drain energy from Earth.

The Cybermen patrol the cold lunar surface.

THE MOONBASE

Written by
Kit Pedler
Featuring
the Second Doctor,
Ben, Polly and Jamie
First broadcast
11 February 1967 –
4 March 1967
4 episodes

The Doctor and his friends arrive on the moon in 2070 to discover that the crew of a moonbase is battling against a strange plague. The base uses a Gravitron to control Earth's weather, and the Cybermen have infected the base's sugar supply to disable the crew. They kidnap and 'alter' victims of the plague before taking over the base.

Ben, Polly and Jamie fight back, destroying the Cybermen with a mixture of solvents that attacks and dissolves their chest units. But many more Cybermen are on the way. The Doctor finally defeats the Cybermen by using the Gravitron to influence the moon's gravity so that the Cybermen and their ships are hurled off into deep space.

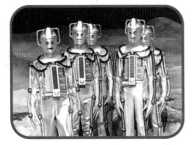

CYBER DATA

The Cybermen that attack the moonbase are of a different design to those of *The Tenth Planet*. The human hands have been replaced with three-fingered metal claws, the chest unit is more streamlined, and the body is a silver suit with cabling and a tubular exoskeleton. The face has changed from a cloth-covered mask to a blank, metal, skull-like helmet. The 'light' is now integrated into the headpiece rather than being separate. A small aerial extends from the chest unit when a Cyberman communicates by radio.

AUGMENTATION

The 'altered' humans that the Cybermen control wear probes attached to their forehead held together in a 'mesh'. When this 'cap' is removed the men become immobile. They are controlled from a box with aerials using a sonic beam, which the Doctor is able to disrupt by altering a tone control on a console. The Cybermen use a cylindrical capsule to transfer humans between their ship and the moonbase without the need for spacesuits.

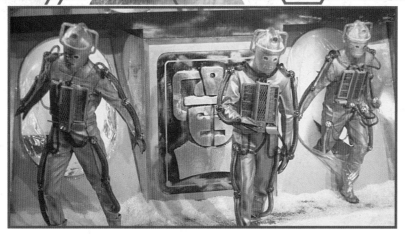

The Cybermen emerge from their frozen tombs.

THE TOMB OF THE CYBERMEN

Arriving on the planet Telos, the Doctor, Jamie and Victoria meet an archaeological expedition led by Professor Parry. His team is planning to excavate the last remains of the Cybermen. They find the Cybermen's city, where the last Cybermen are frozen in huge honeycomb-like tombs below ground. But logicians Kaftan and Klieg plan to revive the Cybermen and form an alliance with them.

Attacked by Cybermats, and with Kaftan's servant, Toberman, part-converted into a Cyberman, the Doctor manages to refreeze the tombs. The Cyber Controller is destroyed as the Doctor booby-traps and closes the doors to the city. He does not see a single Cybermat escape…

Written by
Kit Pedler and Gerry Davis
Featuring
the Second Doctor,
Jamie and Victoria
First broadcast
2 September 1967 –
23 September 1967
4 episodes

CYBERMATS

The Cybermats are small, metallic creatures, not unlike rodents. They have eyes, antennae and a segmented tail. Underneath they move on rows of filaments, and they have what seem to be rows of teeth. They can home in on human brainwaves to attack.

Similar Cybermats, but with spines down their back, no antennae, and solid, unfacetted eyes, are used to attack *The Wheel in Space* and destroy stocks of bernalium there. Their eyes flash when they attack and the Doctor says they have a range of 'at least ten feet'.

In *Revenge of the Cybermen*, the Cybermats disseminate the plague that kills most of the crew of Nerva Beacon. These Cybermats are longer, with segmented bodies and a small red sensor at the front. The Doctor adapts one to attack the Cybermen with gold dust.

CYBER DATA

The Cybermen apparently died out five centuries ago, but nobody knows why. In fact they realised they were in danger of becoming extinct and retreated into their city – which is actually a giant trap.

The control systems form a logic and intelligence test: anyone who passes will revive the Cybermen. They will then be captured and used as raw materials – the first of a new race of Cybermen.

THE CONTROLLER

The Cyber Controller is a taller Cyberman with no chest unit and less piping. His head has an enlarged cranium, lit from within, with visible veins. He lacks the usual 'handles' of the other Cybermen. Like the others, he needs to revitalise himself when his power levels run down. The Doctor tries to trap him inside the large recharging cabinet, but he smashes his way out.

In *Attack of the Cybermen*, we realise the Controller was not destroyed, though he has been redesigned.

THE CYBERMEN

Right: In her very first story, Zoe meets both the Doctor and the Cybermen on the Wheel.

Opposite: Emerging from the sewers, the Cybermen patrol a paralysed London.

THE WHEEL IN SPACE

Written by
David Whitaker,
from a story by Kit Pedler
Featuring
the Second Doctor,
Jamie and Zoe
First broadcast
27 April 1968 –
1 June 1968
6 episodes

The Doctor and Jamie arrive on a spaceship – the *Silver Carrier* – which has apparently drifted off course. They are taken to the nearby Station Three: the Wheel. In fact, the Cybermen have sent the *Silver Carrier*, and are concealed on board. The Cybermen send Cybermats over to the Wheel to destroy the bernalium needed to power the Wheel's X-ray laser.

With a meteorite storm approaching (again, engineered by the Cybermen), the crew of the Wheel find there is bernalium on board the *Silver Carrier* and bring it back to the Wheel. But the Cybermen are concealed inside the crates. The Doctor manages to neutralise the Cybermats and destroy the Cybermen on the Wheel before their main force arrives. The recharged X-ray laser destroys the Cybership.

CYBER DATA

The Cybermen's bodies and external tubing and hydraulics are more streamlined, and the eyes have 'tear-drop' holes at the outside lower corner. There is a similar hole below the mouth.

The Cybermen on the *Silver Carrier* are concealed and preserved inside large egg-like membranes. The Cybermen break out through the shells to operate the Cybermats and put their plans into action. The Cybermats are carried to the Wheel in smaller egg-like bubbles, which sink through the hull.

CYBER PLANNER

The Cybermen are given orders by a Cyber Planner. The Planner is a large bulbous metal object with thin filament attachments within a cradle, not unlike a large stylised Cyberman head mounted on a tiny body.

In *The Invasion* Tobias Vaughn is able to contact the Cybermen via a Cyber Director concealed behind a wall in his office. The Cyber Director seems to have an organic component at the core of a circular electronic structure that turns and pulses with sound and light.

CONTROLLED HUMANS

The Cybermen are able to take control of humans they come into contact with. The Doctor devises a way of resisting this control using a metal plate and resistor taped to the back of the neck.

The Cybermen are able to project mental images from the brain of a controlled Wheel crewman, Vallance. He stares into a control box and thinks of each human being on the Wheel, forming the image in his eyes. The images are then relayed to the Cyber Planner, which advises that 'The Doctor is known and recorded'.

THE INVASION

The Doctor, Jamie and Zoe meet up again with Brigadier Lethbridge-Stewart – now in charge of the newly formed UNIT organisation. UNIT is investigating the world's biggest electronics manufacturer, International Electromatics, and its managing director, Tobias Vaughn.

Vaughn is in league with the Cybermen, who are being shipped to Earth and reanimated at IE's warehouses. They are distributed through the London sewers ready to take over the planet when a hypnotic signal is transmitted through IE's products. With Earth paralysed, the Doctor persuades Vaughn to help defeat the Cybermen. Zoe helps the RAF destroy the Cyber fleet in orbit.

Written by
Derrick Sherwin,
from a story by Kit Pedler
Featuring
the Second Doctor,
Jamie and Zoe
First broadcast
2 November 1968 –
21 December 1968
8 episodes

CYBER DATA

The Cybermen in *The Invasion* are again streamlined, this time with enlarged helmets. They refer to their home (presumably Telos) as 'Planet Fourteen'. Attacked by UNIT forces, the Cybermen are apparently immune to bullets, but can be destroyed with bazookas and grenades.

As in previous stories the Cybermen can control human minds. Major General Rutlidge is under Vaughn's control and warns Vaughn of the Brigadier's attempts to deal with IE.

TOBIAS VAUGHN

Tobias Vaughn, managing director of IE, has a cybernetic body, though he refuses to allow his brain to be altered. When he is shot by Professor Watkins, he simply looks down at the smoking holes in his shirt front, and laughs.

Vaughn eventually agrees to help the Doctor after the Cybermen betray him. They have promised him he will rule Earth, but then they decide to destroy all life with a Cyber megatron bomb.

CEREBRATRON MENTOR

Professor Watkins has developed the Cerebratron Mentor to produce excessively powerful emotional pulses as an aid to learning. But Vaughn intends to mass-produce the machines as a weapon to control the Cybermen after they invade – emotions being alien to the Cybermen. Vaughn tests the machine on one Cyberman, which is driven mad and rampages through the London sewers.

But Vaughn's plans to mass-produce the Cerebratron machines are thwarted when UNIT rescues Watkins.

Right: The Cyberleader and his Cybermen aboard their Cybership.

Opposite: The Cybermen take control of the freighter as it approaches Earth.

REVENGE OF THE CYBERMEN

Written by
Gerry Davis
Featuring
the Fourth Doctor,
Sarah and Harry
First broadcast
19 April 1975 –
10 May 1975
4 episodes

All but a handful of the crew of Nerva Beacon have been wiped out by a plague disseminated by Cybermats. The Doctor realises that Cybermen are close by – hoping to destroy nearby Voga, the Planet of Gold. Gold is lethal to Cybermen, and they must destroy Voga to ensure their survival.

The Doctor is captured and sent down to Voga with two other humans, all three with bombs strapped to them. The Cybemen plan to detonate the bombs to destroy Voga. But when the Doctor defuses the bombs, the Cybermen decide instead to fill Nerva with bombs and crash it into the planet. The Doctor returns to Nerva and prevents the collision, while the Vogans destroy the Cybermen's ship with a missile of their own.

CYBER DATA

The Cybermen who attack Voga have tear-drop eyes and enlarged helmets, and are led by a Cyberleader with a black helmet.

Gold is lethal to Cybermen. It is non-corrodible and coats their breathing apparatus – suffocating them. During the Cyberwar, the humans developed the 'glitter gun' to destroy the Cybermen, using gold from Voga. Now the Cybermen must destroy Voga before they assemble a new Cyber army from parts in their ship and begin another campaign.

VOGA

Voga is the legendary Planet of Gold, all but destroyed by the Cybermen in the Cyberwar. The remains have drifted through space until caught by Jupiter's gravity. The Vogans have survived the journey in a survival chamber built into the caves of Voga.

The leader of the city is Tyrum, while the routes to the surface of Voga are controlled by Vorus and his Guardians. Vorus has secretly worked with a human, Kellman, to lure the Cybermen to Nerva Beacon. Here he plans to destroy them using a Skystriker missile.

EARTHSHOCK

An archaeological team is all but wiped out by strange androids, and the Doctor and his friends are drawn in when they discover the bomb the androids were guarding. The Doctor manages to defuse the bomb, and traces the control signal back to a space freighter en route to Earth.

An army of Cybermen is concealed on board, and emerges to take control. Now that their bomb has been defused they will crash the ship into Earth to destroy a conference forming an alliance against them.

The Cybermen evacuate, and the Doctor and his friends escape. Adric disrupts the controls, and the freighter travels back in time, crashing into prehistoric Earth, causing the extinction of the dinosaurs, but killing Adric.

Written by
Eric Saward
Featuring
the Fifth Doctor,
Adric, Nyssa and Tegan
First broadcast
8 March 1982 –
16 March 1982
4 episodes

DEACTIVATION

On several occasions, Cybermen are deactivated for periods of time, either for preservation or while they are in transit. In *The Tomb of the Cybermen* and *Attack of the Cybermen* (left) we see the ice tombs in their city on Telos, where the Cybermen wait in cryogenic suspension.

In *The Wheel in Space*, they are stored in large egg-like membranes, while in *The Invasion* they are transported to Earth in cotton-wool-like cocoons. In *Earthshock*, the Cybermen stored on the freighter are encased in plastic and revived by a signal from Cyber control.

It is possible that very low temperatures are often used to store the deactivated Cybermen so that the remaining organic elements are preserved along with the mechanical components.

CYBER DATA

These Cybermen are slimmer, with tubing largely built into their bodies rather than built externally. A vestigial chin can be seen moving behind the transparent mouth guard. They are still vulnerable to gold – such as Adric's badge, which the Doctor grinds into the Cyberleader's chest unit.

The Cybermen are led by a Cyberleader, distinguished by the black tubing at the side of its head.

ANDROIDS

Two androids guard the Cyber bomb in the cave system on Earth. They have simple, humanoid forms with featureless oval heads; one seems female and one male. Presumably, as they are referred to as androids, there is no organic material inside them.

The androids fire deadly rays from their hands, but can be destroyed by concentrated blaster fire from Scott's troopers.

A single Raston Warrior Robot destroys a squad of Cybermen.

THE FIVE DOCTORS

Written by
Terrance Dicks
Featuring
the first five Doctors
First UK broadcast
25 November 1983
90-minute TV movie

The first five incarnations of the Doctor and their various companions find themselves brought to the Death Zone on Gallifrey. Here, in ancient times, the Time Lords staged battles between different life forms.

With the Fourth Doctor trapped in a time eddy, the other Doctors make their way to the Dark Tower, battling various creatures including a Dalek and an army of Cybermen along the way. The tower is the tomb of Rassilon – founder of Time Lord society. But corrupt Time Lord President Borusa has been using the Doctors to get him access to the tower so he can claim Rassilon's gift of immortality. However, the gift, when he gets it, is not all he expected and he is incarcerated for ever.

CYBER DATA

The Cybermen in this feature-length, twentieth anniversary **Doctor Who** special are almost identical to those in *Earthshock*. They come up against another creature brought to the Death Zone – a Raston Warrior Robot, one of the most perfect killing machines ever devised. Its armaments are built-in and sensors detect the slightest movement. It produces arrows and blades from its hands, and can teleport itself over short distances. It destroys a team of Cybermen with ruthless efficiency.

THE DEATH ZONE

The Death Zone on Gallifrey is outside time and space. Here the ancient Time Lords gathered alien creatures and forced them to fight as entertainment.

Borusa has drawn several old enemies of the Doctor to the Death Zone to make the Doctor's quest to get to the Dark Tower more interesting. These enemies include a Yeti, a Raston Warrior Robot, a lone Dalek and an army of Cybermen. The Dalek is destroyed when an energy bolt it fires in a reflective corridor is reflected back, destroying it and revealing the thrashing creature inside.

Mercenary Lytton undergoes transformation to become a Cyberman.

ATTACK OF THE CYBERMEN

The Doctor and Peri try to trace a distress call to Earth in 1985. It is from Lytton, who previously worked for the Daleks (see *Resurrection of the Daleks*, page 38), but is now seemingly in league with the Cybermen, who have a base in the London sewers. The Cybermen want to crash Halley's Comet into Earth so that Mondas will not be destroyed in 1986 (see *The Tenth Planet*). They also want to destroy the surface of their own planet, Telos (in the future), to wipe out the native Cryons – who are actually employing Lytton to help steal the Cybermen's time vessel.

The Doctor manages to ignite a store of explosives within the Cyber City, blowing it up, together with the Cybermen and their Controller.

Written by
Paula Moore
Featuring
the Sixth Doctor
and Peri
First broadcast
5 January 1985 –
12 January 1985
2 double-length episodes

CYBER DATA

The Cyber guards patrolling the London sewers are painted black. The Cyberleader on Earth says the Controller was merely damaged when the Doctor sealed him into the booby-trapped Cyber City (see *The Tomb of the Cybermen*).

Cybermen have an in-built distress-call, and will react to the distress of their own kind.

CRYONS

The Cryons, the original inhabitants of Telos, used to live in refrigerated cities before the Cybermen came. They cannot exist in above-freezing conditions; at warmer temperatures they boil and die.

The Cryons have picked up Lytton's distress signal and asked him to help them destroy the Cybermen. They want Lytton to steal the Cybermen's only (captured) time vessel. Without it, the Cybermen cannot avert the destruction of Mondas, so will be forced to stay on Telos and not destroy it.

BATES AND STRATTON

The Cybermen have captured a timeship, which is piloted by a crew of three. Two of the original crew, Bates and Stratton, are part of a working party mining the surface of Telos with an explosive called vastial.

Both Bates and Stratton have been partially converted into Cybermen. Their arms and legs have been replaced with cybernetic ones. Their bodies may be cybernetic or they may be wearing protective suits on the surface of Telos. However, their brains have been unaffected by Cyber conditioning.

The Cybermen emerge from their spaceship.

SILVER NEMESIS

Written by
Kevin Clarke
Featuring
the Seventh Doctor
and Ace
First broadcast
23 November 1988 –
7 December 1988
3 episodes

The Nemesis is a statue of Lady Peinforte made from validium. It was sent into space by the Doctor in 1638 and is now returning to the point where it was launched. When reunited with its bow and arrow it will reach a critical mass. Lady Peinforte wants the power that the statue holds, and travels forward in time from 1638 with the arrow. A group of neo-Nazis also wants it, and they travel from South America with the bow. The Cybermen, too, want the Nemesis, and arrive in force to claim it.

The Doctor activates the statue and seemingly gives it to the Cybermen. But when it reaches their hidden Cyber fleet, the statue explodes and destroys them.

CYBER DATA

Immune to machine-gun fire, the Cybermen are susceptible to gold and are killed by Peinforte's gold-tipped arrows and Ace's gold coins. One Cyberman has a device that detects the gold on Lady Peinforte's arrows. But the Cyberleader detects that Ace has only one coin left without such a device.

With a fleet of thousands of shielded Cyber warships waiting invisibly in space, they plan to use the power of the Nemesis to transform the Earth into their base planet – the new Mondas.

VALIDIUM

Validium is a living metal created as the ultimate defence for Gallifrey by Omega and Rassilon. The Nemesis statue was made by Lady Peinforte in 1638 in her own likeness from validium. The Doctor launched the statue into space in 1638 so the metal could never attain critical mass. For this, the statue needs to be reunited with its bow and arrow.

The Nemesis 'comet' circles the Earth once every 25 years (and generates destruction whenever it comes near).

WALKMEN

The Cybermen have taken over two humans, fitting them with special Cyber-technology headsets. These controlled humans attempt to assassinate the Doctor and Ace.

The Cybermen later kill them for apparent betrayal after Ace destroys the Cybership. The Doctor says the men were transformed by the process – in effect, they were dead already.

CREATING THE CYBERMEN

The Cybermen were the creation of Doctor Kit Pedler, who was a medical researcher when he was recommended to script editor, Gerry Davis, as someone who might be useful as an advisor to **Doctor Who**.

As a doctor, one of Pedler's greatest fears was 'dehumanising medicine'. He foresaw a time when spare-part surgery reached the stage where it was commonplace, even cosmetic. He feared that there would come a point where it was impossible to tell how much of the original human being remained. The resulting Cybermen, he thought, would be motivated by pure logic, coupled with the overriding desire to survive. They would sacrifice their entire bodies and their minds in the quest for immortality.

Costume supervisor, Sandra Reid, had the job of creating the first Cybermen. Although the look of the Cybermen would change and evolve almost with every story in which they appeared, the initial design included the main elements that make the Cybermen recognisable: the blank mask-like face, 'jug handles' connected to a light in the head, cables and rods to enhance the limbs, and the large chest unit.

SCRIPT EXTRACTS - *THE TENTH PLANET*

```
The sleeve on the arm of one of them
slips back. Instead of flesh there is a
transparent 'arm-shaped' forearm contain-
ing shining rods and lights. There is a
normal hand at the end of it. A close-up
of one of their heads reveals a metal
plate running between centre hairline
front and occiput...
```

```
They are tall, slim with one-piece close-
fitting silver mesh uniform. Their faces
and hands are normal but under the hair
on the head is a long shining metal plate
stretching from centre hairline front to
occiput. (This could be disguised by a
hat.) Their faces are all rather alike,
angular and normally good-looking. On the
front of their trunks is a mechanical
(computer-like) unit, consisting of
switches, two rows of lights, and a short
moveable proboscis. They carry (exotic)
side arms. At elbow joints and shoulders
there are small ram-like cylinders acting
over the joints.
```

THE DALEKS

The Daleks are the most hated and feared life form in the universe. Originally from the planet Skaro, their empire now covers much of known space. While they appear to be armoured robots, the casing is really the survival chamber for the hideous creature inside.

The mutated Dalek creatures are the end result of a thousand-year war between the Kaleds and the Thals. A Kaled scientist, Davros, experimented to discover the ultimate mutated form of his race, and designed the Dalek travel machine to enable the resultant creatures to survive. Now dependent on radiation, and powered by static electricity, the Daleks' only ambition is the conquest of all other life forms and the total extermination of their enemies.

Luminosity dischargers light up when the Dalek speaks

Data from the Dalek's eye is transferred directly into the brain of the Dalek creature

The sucker cup can manipulate objects and be used as a weapon. It produces a tremendously powerful vacuum

The main chamber is where the Dalek creature is housed within the casing – floating in a nutrient-rich fluid, and attached directly by positronic linkages into the various on-board systems

The Dalek's gun can be set to various levels of destructive capability

Some of these globes replace the external sense organs, while others contain additional capabilities including high explosive charges for offensive action or self-destruct

The gyroscopic stabilisation system enables the Dalek to remain upright even in adverse circumstances

The casing of the Dalek is made from an incredibly tough and durable metal called dalekenium

The Dalek's motive power system. Away from Skaro (see page 27), static electrical power is generated from energy absorbed by the power slats below the dome

HIERARCHY OF THE DALEKS

While the colour schemes of ordinary Daleks vary, there is a distinct hierarchy to their ranks, and Daleks instinctively recognise their superiors and subordinates. A supreme council commands the Daleks, headed by the Supreme Dalek and answerable to the Emperor.

One faction of Daleks, in later times, answers to their creator, Davros, and is opposed to the Daleks loyal to the Supreme Dalek. Davros, at some point, takes over as Emperor, as we discover in *Remembrance of the Daleks*.

The Doctor and his companions encounter the Daleks for the first time.

THE DALEKS

The TARDIS arrives on Skaro, a planet all-but destroyed by a thousand-year war that ended with the detonation of an immensely powerful neutron bomb. In a huge metal city, left intact by the bomb, the Doctor and his companions discover the Daleks – hideously mutated survivors of the war, kept alive inside metal war machines powered by static electricity, and dependent upon the radioactivity in the atmosphere. The Daleks are determined to wipe out the Thals – their opponents in the war, now mutated into perfect blond-haired humans. The Doctor persuades the pacifist Thals to attack the Dalek City and defeat the creatures before they can release radioactive waste into the atmosphere.

Written by
Terry Nation
Featuring
the First Doctor, Ian, Barbara and Susan
First broadcast
21 December 1963 –
1 February 1964
7 episodes

DALEK DATA

The Daleks of this story are of a uniform, metallic silver appearance. They are powered by static electricity, which they pick up from the metal floor of their city, and they cannot travel beyond its limits. They have a xenophobic hatred of the Thals and are determined to exterminate them.

SKARO

The planet Skaro, the twelfth planet in its solar system, has been laid waste by the war, which ended centuries ago. The only surviving structure seems to be the Dalek City, which stands in a desert close to the Petrified Jungle. Here the intense heat of the neutron bomb has turned the soil to ash and the trees and flowers to brittle stone.

Behind the city is a range of mountains, and then the Lake of Mutations – named after the hideous and deadly mutated monsters that survive in its glowing waters.

THE THALS

In the centuries since the war, the Thals have mutated due to the radioactive fall-out and the residue of chemical and biological weapons. But unlike the Daleks, their mutation has come full circle. Now they are a race of tall, Aryan humanoids. Because of their history they are staunchly pacifist, refusing to fight the Daleks, even though they know this means they will die.

THE DALEKS

THE DALEK INVASION OF EARTH

Written by
Terry Nation
Featuring
the First Doctor, Ian,
Barbara and Susan
First broadcast
21 November 1964 –
26 December 1964
6 episodes

In 2157, the Daleks invade Earth. Their plan is to drill through Earth's crust and blow out the planet's core with a penetration explosive capsule. They will then install a guidance system so as to pilot the Earth like a giant spaceship.

The Doctor and his companions arrive in a devastated London and help the human resistance fighters to oppose the Daleks. But after an attack on the main Dalek landing site goes disastrously wrong, they have to escape from London. They make their separate ways to the Daleks' main mining operations in Bedfordshire, where the Doctor and his friends manage to divert the Dalek bomb intended to blow open the Earth.

DALEK DATA

The Daleks in this story can now travel outside the confines of their city, invading other worlds. They have enlarged 'fenders', and pick up power through a receiver dish on the back of their casing. The base of a Dalek is seen to be flat, when it is lifted by rebelling miners.

They are led by the Black Dalek – also called the 'Supreme Controller'. There is also mention of a separate 'Supreme Command'. The Saucer Commander is seen, a predominantly black Dalek, but with alternating black and silver flanges on its base section.

ROBOMEN

Because there are relatively few Daleks on Earth, they operate on intelligent prisoners and turn them into living robots – Robomen. The so-called 'transfer' operation controls the human brain, at least for a time. But after a while, the processing breaks down and the Robomen go insane and kill themselves.

The Daleks relay instructions to the Robomen through a helmet grafted onto the skull that picks up high-frequency radio waves. The helmet flashes when in communication, and the Daleks always know when a Roboman is attacked.

THE SLYTHER

The revolting Slyther is a 'pet' of the Black Dalek, used to enforce the curfew at the Dalek mine in Bedfordshire. It roams the mine area at night in search of food – humans. The Slyther's horrific, screaming cries strike terror into the mine workers.

The Slyther is killed when it falls into a mine shaft while attacking Ian and his friend Larry Madison as they hide from the Daleks.

Left: The Daleks battle the robotic Mechonoids.

Opposite: Daleks patrol London – deserted after their conquest.

THE CHASE

The Dalek Supreme sends an execution squad to pursue the Doctor and his companions through time and space. They almost catch the Doctor on the desert planet of Aridius, but the TARDIS escapes first to the Empire State Building, then the *Mary Celeste*, where the Daleks terrify the crew into abandoning ship. After a narrow escape from an apparently haunted house, the Daleks corner the time travellers on Mechanus.

Here the Doctor and his friends are captured by the robot Mechonoids. When the Daleks arrive, there is a pitched battle between Mechonoids and Daleks. As it rages, the Doctor and his friends escape – Ian and Barbara taking the Daleks' time machine to get home to sixties London.

Written by
Terry Nation
Featuring
the First Doctor, Ian, Barbara and Vicki
First broadcast
22 May 1965 –
26 June 1965
6 episodes

DALEK DATA

The Daleks in this story have vertical slats over the bands round their mid-section, like armour-plating. This basic design remains fundamentally unchanged over the coming years.

The Daleks know of the Mechonoids, and they are able to create a robot duplicate of the Doctor to trick his companions – though it assumes (from previous encounters) that the young girl with the Doctor is Susan, whereas in fact she is Vicki, enabling Ian to spot which Doctor is who!

DALEK TIME TRAVEL

For the first time we see the Daleks travel through time. They also use a time machine, which is bigger inside than out, in *The Daleks' Master Plan*. In other stories they use either small, portable time machines – as in *Day of the Daleks* – or 'time corridors' that link specific times and places. In *The Evil of the Daleks*, they have a time corridor from Skaro to Maxtible's house in 1866, and from there to London in 1966. In *Resurrection of the Daleks*, a time corridor links the Dalek ship in the future with a warehouse in London in 1984.

THE MECHONOIDS

The Mechonoids are robots sent from Earth to prepare the planet Mechanus for colonisation. They have built a city on huge stilts, 1500 feet above the jungle of Mechanus, and wait for the colonists, who, because of interplanetary wars, will never come.

But until human immigrants with the right control codes arrive, they treat all other life forms as specimens for study, or enemies to be destroyed with their flame-thrower weaponry. Weakened by fire, their city collapses when the Daleks attack.

THE DALEKS' MASTER PLAN

Written by
Terry Nation and
Dennis Spooner
Featuring
the First Doctor, Steven and
Katarina, with Sara Kingdom
First broadcast
13 November 1965 –
29 January 1966
12 episodes

Following on from *Mission to the Unknown* (see below), the Daleks' plan for conquest is nearing completion when the treacherous Guardian of the Solar System – Mavic Chen – delivers the taranium core of their Time Destructor to Kembel. But the Doctor manages to steal the taranium and escape in Chen's ship. The Daleks and Chen pursue the Doctor and his friends through space and time, from the prison planet Desperus to ancient Egypt. The Doctor tries to keep the taranium from the Daleks. Finally, back on Kembel, the Doctor operates the Time Destructor and destroys them.

MISSION TO THE UNKNOWN

In a single-episode story that does not feature the Doctor, Space Agent Marc Cory is investigating the sighting of a Dalek ship in the year 4000. He soon discovers they have a base on the planet Kembel. But his crew are infected by homicidal Varga plants, imported from Skaro, and they themselves start to mutate into deadly Vargas. Elsewhere on Kembel, the Daleks are negotiating with representatives of the six outer galaxies to destroy the solar system. Cory records a message of warning, but before he can send it he is found and exterminated.

THE DALEK DELEGATES

The members of the Dalek Alliance (except Mavic Chen) are the rulers of the outer galaxies: Sentreal; Zephon, Master of the Fifth Galaxy; the Masters of Celation and Beaus; Trantis, the representative of the largest of the outer galaxies; Malpha and Gearon.

Mavic Chen is the Guardian of the Solar System. Not content merely to rule Earth's galaxy, Chen plans to betray the Daleks and take control with a fleet of Earth security vessels. But the Daleks are just as perfidious, and they exterminate Chen before he can betray them.

SPECIAL SPACE SECURITY

The SSS is Earth's elite defence and security force. Its top agents include Marc Cory – exterminated by the Daleks on Kembel – and Bret Vyon, who was sent to find Cory. He too is killed – branded a traitor by Mavic Chen and assassinated by his own sister, Agent Sara Kingdom. After the Doctor proves to Sara that Vyon was innocent, she helps the Doctor and Steven to destroy the Daleks, even at the cost of her own life. She ages to death on Kembel when the Time Destructor is activated.

Left: Two deactivated Daleks in their crashed capsule.

Opposite: The Daleks and their allies make plans for universal conquest.

THE POWER OF THE DALEKS

On the Earth colony Vulcan, a space capsule is recovered after being buried for over 200 years in a mercury swamp. Inside, scientist Lesterson discovers three inert Daleks. Not knowing what they are, he reactivates one. The newly regenerated Doctor and his friends struggle to convince the colonists that the (disarmed) Daleks are not harmless, friendly or servile. But then a rebel group tries to use the Daleks to help them seize power. As the humans fight each other, the Daleks have set up a secret facility to create a Dalek army, which emerges from the capsule to exterminate all humans! But the Doctor manages to turn their power source against them and the Daleks are destroyed. Or are they?

Written by
David Whitaker
Featuring
the Second Doctor,
Ben and Polly
First broadcast
5 November 1966 –
10 December 1966
6 episodes

DALEK DATA

Disarmed by the scientist Lesterson, the Daleks are forced to operate from a position of weakness. They scheme throughout to get the power supply that will place them in a dominant position from which they can destroy the colony.

When their weapons are returned, their firepower is as awesome as ever. One Dalek gun fires through two-inch-thick tungsten steel by way of demonstration to the rebel leaders.

DALEK PRODUCTION LINE

The three Daleks in the capsule set up a conveyor-belt production line to make empty casings into which the Dalek creatures are placed. The top section of the Dalek is then lowered into place and the complete Dalek emerges ready to do battle with the human colonists. The Dalek creatures may have been stored in the secret area of the capsule, or may have been manufactured or bred specifically when needed.

STATIC POWER

The Daleks can store power, but they require a static electrical circuit for permanent energy. The Doctor likens static power to their blood: 'a constant life-stream'. In The Daleks, the metal floors were wired to provide the Daleks with power; they could not leave their city. In The Dalek Invasion of Earth, the Daleks picked up power through receiver dishes attached to their backs. The slats over the Daleks middle sections store and supply power.

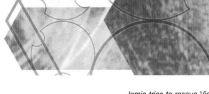

Jamie tries to rescue Victoria from the Daleks.

THE EVIL OF THE DALEKS

Written by
David Whitaker
Featuring
the Second Doctor,
Jamie and Victoria
First broadcast
20 May 1967 –
1 July 1967
7 episodes

The Daleks steal the TARDIS and lure the Doctor and Jamie to scientist Theodore Maxtible's house near Canterbury in 1866. Here Jamie is tested by having to rescue Victoria (the daughter of another scientist) while his emotions are recorded. The Daleks want to distil 'the Human Factor', which will show why humans have always defeated them.

Back on Skaro, the Emperor Dalek reveals that the Doctor has refined the Dalek Factor – the impulse to exterminate – which they will spread through Earth history. But the Doctor 'infects' some Daleks with the Human Factor and they begin to question the orders of their leaders. With a Dalek civil war raging, the Doctor, Jamie and Victoria escape.

DALEK DATA

The Daleks are commanded by black Dalek Leaders, with a black dome and mid-section. These are the Emperor's guards, and they battle the humanised Daleks to protect the Emperor. When the top is blown off a Dalek in the civil war, a glutinous gunge erupts from inside its casing, which may issue from the Dalek creature's protective environment.

The Doctor explains that the Dalek City is huge, mainly below ground. Within the city we see the Emperor's throne room and various other facilities including the weapon shop.

THE EMPEROR DALEK

The Daleks' supreme leader is the Emperor – a massive Dalek built into the very fabric of the Dalek City on Skaro. Despite the Doctor's assertion that this is the 'final end' of the Daleks, the Emperor is not totally destroyed in the civil war.

In *Remembrance of the Daleks*, the Emperor Dalek is a 'normal' Dalek with an enlarged globe replacing the top section, and no eye stalk. This turns out to be Davros.

ALPHA, BETA, OMEGA

Once revived, the three test Daleks in which the Doctor implants the Human Factor are just like children. The Doctor says they will grow up quickly, and names them Alpha, Beta and Omega. In their childlike state, the test Daleks play 'trains' and spin the Doctor round as he rides on their fenders. 'Dizzy Doctor', they intone with glee, and sing their new names. The Doctor strikes up a bizarre friendship with the three Daleks.

The Doctor finds himself in a terrifying alternative future where the Daleks have invaded Earth.

DAY OF THE DALEKS

The Doctor investigates a mysterious attack on diplomat Sir Reginald Styles, and discovers that guerrillas from the twenty-second century are trying to assassinate him. They believe Styles sabotaged a peace conference in their past – our present – and the resulting wars gave the Daleks the chance to invade Earth.

In the Dalek-ruled future, the Doctor and Jo struggle to avoid capture and to learn what really happened. But as the Doctor returns to put history back on track, the Daleks – and their ape-like servants the Ogrons – prepare their own attack on the conference. The Daleks are finally destroyed when one of the guerrillas blows up Sir Reginald's house.

Written by
Louis Marks
Featuring
the Third Doctor,
UNIT and Jo
First broadcast
1 January 1972 –
22 January 1972
4 episodes

DALEK DATA

From now on, the Dalek eyes have a black 'pupil' rather than a solid white disc. The chief Dalek is gold, and the other Daleks are dark grey. The Daleks use their Mind Analysis Machine to establish the Doctor's identity.

Bullets and mortars have no apparent effect on Daleks during their attack on Auderly House.

OGRONS

The ape-like Ogrons are a form of higher anthropoid that used to live in scattered communities on one of the outer planets. The Daleks use them to supplement human security forces. They are very simple, very honest, very loyal, and very strong. Apparently immune to the Doctor's Venusian karate, one Ogron is felled by a blow to the head with a carafe of wine.

The Ogrons are seen to be working for the Daleks again, under the guidance of the Master, in *Frontier in Space*.

AN ALTERNATIVE INVASION

The Daleks have managed to invade because of a time paradox. The Doctor discovers that the peace conference was not destroyed by Styles, but by one of the future guerrilla fighters trying to assassinate Styles to prevent the very war this causes.

Under Dalek rule, Earth is run like a giant labour camp, its raw materials mined and taken to Skaro to supply the expanding Dalek empire.

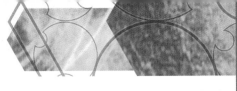

The Doctor and the Thal leader, Taron, struggle with a Dalek.

PLANET OF THE DALEKS

Written by
Terry Nation
Featuring
the Third Doctor
and Jo
First broadcast
7 April 1973 –
12 May 1973
6 episodes

The Doctor and Jo follow a group of Daleks to the planet Spiridon. Here they find a group of Thals (see page 27) on a suicide mission to prevent the Daleks learning how to be invisible. (The Daleks are studying the native – invisible – Spiridons, who they have enslaved.) The Thals believe there are only a dozen Daleks on the planet, but the Doctor discovers a massive Dalek army held in suspended animation in an ice cavern.

As the Daleks prepare to unleash a deadly bacteria to destroy the Thals, the Doctor and his friends fight their way into the Dalek base. They manage to flood the army with liquid ice, freezing it for centuries.

DALEK DATA

Most Daleks have an automatic distress transmitter, which may be activated if the casing is opened, even after the Dalek is deactivated. Spiridon has been totally subjugated with the usual Dalek technique, which the Doctor describes as, 'mass exterminations, followed by absolute suppression of the survivors'.

The Daleks' guidance system uses high-frequency radio impulses, which the Doctor manages to jam to confuse one Dalek. The cold of the Spiridon night slows the Daleks' mechanical reflexes – they hardly function at all at sub-zero.

INVISIBLE DALEKS

From studying the Spiridons, the Daleks have discovered an anti-reflecting light wave that enables them to become invisible. But as generating the wave takes enormous power, they can only stay invisible for short periods. Some of the Daleks suffer from light-wave sickness as a side effect and deactivate.

THE DALEK SUPREME

The Black Dalek in early Dalek stories was also referred to as the Dalek Supreme. In this story, it is seen to be black and gold with enlarged dome lights and is said to be 'one of the Supreme Council'. There is mention of a ruling council in *The Daleks*.

The Supreme Dalek is referred to in later stories – including *Destiny of the Daleks* and *Revelation of the Daleks* – opposed to Davros. A Supreme Dalek also appears in *Resurrection of the Daleks* and as leader of the rebel Daleks in *Remembrance of the Daleks*.

Primitive Exxilons manage to destroy a weakened Dalek.

DEATH TO THE DALEKS

The TARDIS loses power when it lands on Exxilon. The Doctor meets up with a stranded group of humans mining for parrinium, the antidote to a space plague. Sarah finds a huge city, but is captured by native Exxilons. A group of Daleks arrives, also apparently looking for parrinium. They too lose power and their guns fail, forcing them into an uneasy alliance with the humans. But the Daleks are planning to take all the parrinium.

Equipped with machine guns, the Daleks take over. Meanwhile, the Doctor and a rebel Exxilon, Bellal, enter the city, the source of the power drain. They destroy it, but the Dalek ship leaves as power is restored. It is destroyed by Galloway, one of the humans, using a Dalek bomb.

Written by
Terry Nation
Featuring
the Third Doctor
and Sarah
First broadcast
23 February 1974 –
16 March 1974
4 episodes

DALEK VOICES

As recognisable as the Dalek's distinctive pepperpot shape is its grating metallic voice. This was created by treating the actor's voice with a 'ring modulator', which adds and subtracts an input signal's frequency (in this case the actor doing the Dalek voice) from an

internal oscillator's frequency. Unfortunately, the frequency used was never noted, and so Dalek voices tended to alter between stories.

The earliest Dalek voices were provided by Peter Hawkins – a well-known voice artist. He was joined by David Graham – a regular voice actor for Gerry Anderson. Later, Roy Skelton provided Dalek voices, as did Michael Wisher (above), who was also the original Davros. Other actors have also given voice to the Daleks – most notable in recent times being Nicholas Briggs (left), who

also wrote and directed the audio CD series *Dalek Empire*. A talented writer, actor and voice artist (as well as a massive fan of the Daleks), Nick provides voices for the Daleks in the new series of **Doctor Who**, as well as other creatures including the Nestene Consciousness (see page 5) and the Adherents of the Repeated Meme (see page 59).

DALEK DATA

The Doctor says that the Daleks move by psycho-kinetic power, which is why only their armaments and spaceship are affected by the power loss. Inside each Dalek, the Doctor says, is a 'living, bubbling lump of hate'.

One Dalek survives an electric shock of 7000 volts inside Exxilon City, while another self-destructs when it 'fails' by letting a prisoner escape. While usually fitted with a standard gun, in *Death to the Daleks*, they replace their inactive blasters with machine guns, which they describe as 'moderately efficient'.

THE DALEKS

Right: Davros demonstrates the very first Dalek.

Opposite: The Daleks capture Romana.

GENESIS OF THE DALEKS

Written by
Terry Nation
Featuring
the Fourth Doctor,
Sarah and Harry
First broadcast
8 March 1975 –
12 April 1975
6 episodes

The Time Lords despatch the Doctor to Skaro in the distant past to avert the creation of the Daleks. He arrives at the end of a thousand-year war between the Thals and the Kaleds. Anyone mutated by the chemical and biological weapons is banished outside their huge domed cities, and crippled Kaled scientist Davros has realised the mutation process is irreversible. So he has invented a 'travel machine' that will ensure the survival of the creature he knows his race will become – the Dalek.

But he makes the Daleks ambitious creatures of hate, without feeling or pity for inferior life forms. The Doctor manages to slow Dalek development, but leaves as the Daleks take over Skaro and exterminate Davros.

DALEK DATA

Davros calls his prototype Dalek a Mark III Travel Machine. All the Daleks he creates are gunmetal grey in colour. The first Dalek is able to detect that the Doctor and Harry are aliens.

It is impossible to know at what point the Daleks decide they no longer need Davros. Once they have secured the Kaled Elite's bunker, they start up the automated Dalek production line Davros has set up – and when his henchman, Nyder, tries to stop it, they exterminate him.

DALEK ORIGINS

While *Genesis of the Daleks* is the definitive account of the creation of the Daleks, the *TV Century 21* Dalek comic strip of 1965 gave another account. The Daleks here were war machines developed by Yarvelling of the short, warlike, blue-skinned Dalek race. The Daleks plan to destroy the Thals with a neutron bomb, which is prematurely detonated by a meteorite storm, and two years later, Yarvelling's dying action is to adapt his war machine to carry the mutated remains of his people.

DAVROS

Crippled and deformed, Davros is part-way to becoming a Dalek himself. His wheelchair is the base of a Dalek, his voice electronically modified and enhanced so that it sounds like a Dalek. Davros is the head of the Kaled's Elite Scientific Corps – a group of the best scientists, headquartered in a bunker some miles from the main Kaled dome.

A brilliant scientist and ruthless politician, Davros will stop at nothing to ensure the completion and success of his Dalek project.

DESTINY OF THE DALEKS

The Doctor and Romana arrive on Skaro where they meet the Movellans, who are locked in a stalemate in their war against the Daleks. The Daleks are digging through the remains of their ancient city to find and revive Davros, in the hope he can give them an advantage in their war.

The Movellans are a robot race, and they hope the Doctor can give them a similar advantage. The Doctor captures Davros, but the Daleks exterminate their human slave-workers until the Doctor surrenders. As the Movellans prepare to depart and destroy the planet, the Doctor frees the slave-workers to take over their ship. He tricks Davros into destroying the approaching 'suicide' Daleks and Davros is taken to Earth for trial.

Written by
Terry Nation
Featuring
the Fourth Doctor
and Romana
First broadcast
1 September 1979 –
22 September 1979
4 episodes

DALEK DATA

Davros was not destroyed, it seems, but went into suspended animation after being shot by the Daleks in *Genesis of the Daleks*. The Daleks believe he can help them defeat the Movellans, and are willing to sacrifice themselves, if need be, to rescue him. A group of Daleks strap explosives to their armour, which will be detonated when they close in on the Movellan ship – destroying themselves and their enemy.

THE MOVELLANS

The Movellans appear to be beautiful humanoids. In fact they are ruthless robots, locked in a war with the Daleks. But the battle computers of both fleets are so evenly matched they anticipate and neutralise the other's every move.

Led by Commander Sharrel, the Movellans believe the Doctor can solve this stalemate – which he can: whichever side turns off its battle computers will become unpredictable and win the war.

The Doctor is able to disrupt the Movellans' control systems with his K-9 dog whistle.

CREATING DAVROS

Terry Nation's script for *Genesis of the Daleks* described Davros as having a wheelchair 'not unlike' the base of a Dalek, while sculptor John Friedlander based his mask partly on the evil Mekon from the *Eagle*'s Dan Dare comic strip.

Interviewed after *Destiny of the Daleks* aired, Nation said: 'Davros served two roles. Firstly he was half-man, half-Dalek, a sort of mutated missing link. Secondly, I wanted someone who could think like a Dalek, but talk in a more human fashion. I feel the Daleks themselves should be left to speak in short, snappy sentences.'

Can the Doctor bring himself to execute Davros?

RESURRECTION OF THE DALEKS

Written by
Eric Saward
Featuring
the Fifth Doctor,
Tegan and Turlough
First broadcast
8 February 1984 –
15 February 1984
2 double-length episodes

Ninety years after Davros was imprisoned in suspended animation, the Daleks come to free him. The Movellans have won the war, developing a deadly Dalek virus. The Daleks need Davros – to find an antidote.

The Doctor and his friends find samples of the virus in a warehouse in present-day London. The Daleks capture the Doctor by means of a time corridor linking London in 1984 to their ship. They intend to duplicate him and send him to assassinate the Time Lord High Council. But as Davros betrays the Dalek Supreme and turns his own Daleks against him, the virus is unleashed – which also affects Davros. The Dalek ship is destroyed by a Dalek 'duplicate' human who reverts to his true nature.

DALEK DATA

The Daleks are able to duplicate humans – including a bomb-disposal squad sent to investigate the canisters of virus stored in a warehouse in London. The Dalek Supreme claims that Dalek duplicates now occupy key positions on twentieth-century Earth.

Davros has a device concealed in his chair that enables him to take over humans and even Daleks. Planning to destroy the Daleks and start again with his Dalek project, Davros releases the virus – only to find it affects him too.

DALEK CREATURES

Until the episode *Dalek* in the 2005 series, the creature inside the Dalek had rarely been revealed, but we had seen glimpses. In *The Daleks*, a four-fingered claw emerges from under a Thal cape where the Doctor and Ian have dumped the creature from inside one Dalek. Dalek embryos are seen as green, sponge-like creatures in *Genesis of the Daleks*. 'Young' Dalek creatures, writhing with tentacles, are placed inside Daleks on the production line in *The Power of the Daleks*, and in *Resurrection of the Daleks* a Dalek creature escapes from its destroyed casing before being shot by the Doctor and his friends.

When a Dalek is destroyed, in *The Evil of the Daleks*, the pulsing, writhing gunge inside is revealed. In *The Five Doctors* and *Resurrection of the Daleks* (right), the dead Daleks are seen. And in *Revelation of the Daleks*, Natasha finds her father, Stengos – or rather just his head – being mutated into a new Dalek creature by Davros.

The Daleks arrive at Tranquil Repose looking for Davros.

REVELATION OF THE DALEKS

Tranquil Repose is a cemetery where those with incurable diseases can be cryogenically frozen to await a cure for their ailment. But the 'Great Healer' in charge is actually Davros. He is building a new army of Daleks from the most intelligent cryogenic sleepers, and using the rest to create concentrated food protein, which is saving the galaxy from starvation.

Davros lures the Doctor to Tranquil Repose to exact his revenge. But the double-crossing Kara has also sent an assassin, Orcini, to kill Davros. The Doctor and Peri escape as a group of Daleks loyal to the Dalek Supreme arrive to capture Davros and take him back to Skaro for trial. Orcini detonates a bomb, sacrificing himself to destroy Davros's army.

Written by
Eric Saward
Featuring
the Sixth Doctor
and Peri
First broadcast
23 March 1985 –
30 March 1985
2 double-length episodes

DALEK DATA

Davros is mutating the humans at Tranquil Repose into Dalek creatures. The creatures' brains are cultivated in incubators, then transplanted into nascent, transparent Daleks that grow into 'adult' machine-creatures. Davros's Daleks are ivory coloured, with gold sense-spheres and 'trim'.

The Skaro Daleks easily defeat Davros's new Daleks in battle, and are going to put Davros on trial for crimes against the Daleks. They plan to recondition Davros's Daleks to obey the Dalek Supreme.

TRANQUIL REPOSE

Tranquil Repose is a cemetery combined with a facility where the terminally ill, amongst others, can be cryogenically suspended until a later date – for example when a cure for their ailment is discovered. A local DJ provides a 'personalised entertainment system'.

However, the theory does not work, as in practice nobody wants the cryogenically suspended people back – in many cases they would be in conflict with those currently in power. Also, the galaxy can barely support the current population.

ORCINI

Temporarily excommunicated from the Grand Order of Oberon, Orcini is a feared assassin. It is said he has only to breathe on a victim for him to die. He has an artificial leg with a faulty hydraulic valve (the leg is blown off by a blast from a Dalek gun). When he is seated, the valve is inclined to jam – but he refuses to have it fixed as it is a constant reminder of his own mortality. He lost his leg the one time he did not listen to the instincts of his squire, Bostock. To cleanse his conscience he gives his fee to charity.

The Doctor meets the Imperial Daleks.

REMEMBRANCE OF THE DALEKS

Written by
Ben Aaronovitch
Featuring
the Seventh Doctor
and Ace
First broadcast
5 October 1988 –
26 October 1988
4 episodes

The Doctor and Ace arrive in London in 1963, where the Doctor left the so-called Hand of Omega for safety. But now two groups of Daleks are after this powerful device, which can be used for manipulating stars. Imperial Daleks, led by their Emperor, battle against 'Rebel' Daleks led by the Dalek Supreme. The Doctor teams up with a military unit led by Group Captain Gilmore to destroy both factions. The Imperial Daleks win the battle, using their Special Weapons Dalek. The Emperor is revealed to be Davros – who uses the Hand of Omega despite the Doctor's warnings. But the Doctor has tricked Davros, and the device destroys first Skaro, and then the Imperial Dalek mothership over Earth.

DALEK DATA

The Imperial Daleks are an ivory colour with gold 'trim'. Their slats are moulded into the bodywork rather than attached, and the eye and sucker arm are of a different design. The Dalek creatures are different too – a claw emerges to attack the Doctor, and they have functional appendages and mechanical prostheses grafted on. They are led by the Emperor – a Dalek with a spherical head – which is revealed to contain Davros.

The Rebel Dalek faction is led by the black-and-silver Dalek Supreme. These Daleks are of a gunmetal-grey design.

SPECIAL WEAPONS DALEK

The Special Weapons Dalek is battle-marked, with no eye stalk or sucker arm and an enlarged gun. Until it is ordered into action, the Imperial Daleks are losing to the Rebel faction.

The Rebel Daleks have projected-energy weapons that leave no tissue damage but scramble the victim's insides.

DALEK BATTLE COMPUTER

The Dalek battle computer is a Dalek base with headset attached – a bio-mechanoid control device for a young human. The Doctor explains that the Daleks' major drawback is their dependency on rationality and logic, and the solution is to get a human – preferably young and imaginative – plug them into the system and slave their ingenuity and creativity to the battle computer. In this case the human is a young schoolgirl. She recovers after the Dalek Supreme is destroyed.

CREATING THE FIRST DALEKS

In 1963, **Doctor Who**'s story editor, David Whitaker, asked Terry Nation to write the second-ever **Doctor Who** story – the result was *The Daleks*, and **Doctor Who** would never be the same again.

The descriptions of the Daleks in Terry Nation's scripts gave little idea of the tremendous visual impact his monsters would achieve. The first appearance of a Dalek was at the end of Episode 1, where the sucker arm is seen as it menaces Barbara:

```
SEEN ONLY BY THE AUDIENCE, A
PANEL SLIDES OPEN AND THERE
EMERGES FROM IT A PAIR OF
MECHANICAL ARMS.
BARBARA HEARS THE SOUND BEHIND
HER AND TURNS IN TIME TO SEE THE
THING THAT IS ADVANCING ON HER.
ONLY ITS ARMS ARE SEEN BY THE
AUDIENCE AS THEY PIN BARBARA'S
ARM TO HER SIDE AND SHE STARTS TO
SCREAM.
```

Later, in Episode 2, the Daleks were fully revealed:

```
STANDING IN A HALF CIRCLE IN
FRONT OF THEM ARE FOUR HIDEOUS
MACHINE-LIKE CREATURES. THEY ARE
LEGLESS, MOVING ON A ROUND BASE.
THEY HAVE NO HUMAN FEATURES.
A LENS ON A FLEXIBLE SHAFT ACTS
AS AN EYE.
ARMS WITH MECHANICAL GRIPS FOR
HANDS(WE HAVE SEEN THESE ARMS
BEFORE, MOVING UP BEHIND BARBARA).
THE CREATURES HOLD STRANGE
WEAPONS IN THEIR HANDS.
ONE OF THEM GLIDES FORWARD. IT
SPEAKS WITH AN ECHOING METALLIC
VOICE.
```

It was the job of BBC designer Raymond Cusick to bring these descriptions to life. Cusick based his design around the shape of a man sitting on a chair. To this basic shape he added the sucker arm and gun (originally at different levels) and an eye at the top of the creature. The job of building the four Dalek machines was subcontracted to a company called Shawcraft Models.

Despite slight modifications for later stories – most notably the addition of 'slats' over the mid-section bands – the basic design of the Daleks has remained unchanged and is immediately recognised around the world.

Raymond Cusick's original sketches of the Daleks (above) and an ivory-and-gold Imperial Dalek.

THE DALEKS

REINVENTING THE DALEKS

With the new series of **Doctor Who**, the Doctor's oldest and deadliest foes – the Daleks – are back.

The task of re-imagining the Daleks for the twenty-first century was embraced by the series' design team, who welcomed the challenge. Led by production designer Edward Thomas, the team set about reinventing the Dalek. Right from the beginning they were determined that the overall shape and instantly recognisable image of the Dalek should remain basically the same. This would be a revision, an improvement on the original design, rather than a complete reinvention.

A measure of the team's success was that within hours of its (supposedly secret) filming debut at Cardiff's Millennium Stadium, the new Dalek had its own full-page spread in the *Sun*.

Right: Matthew Savage's final concept painting for the new Dalek.

Below: The resulting design from which the Dalek was built.

DALEK DESIGN

Shown here for the first time are some of the original design ideas for the new Dalek, created by concept designer Matthew Savage.

Right: A design for the rear of the imprisoned Dalek.

Far right: The Dalek in its cell, gun removed and flesh pulled through its casing.

HOW TO BUILD A DALEK

Two complete Daleks were actually built for the episode *Dalek* – one highly damaged Dalek, and one in pristine condition. Working from Matthew Savage's original concept drawings and paintings, Mike Tucker (**Doctor Who**'s models and miniatures supervisor) and his team set about the task of recreating an iconic monster. Using elements from the original sixties Daleks, they updated and improved the design using state-of-the-art materials and technology.

The original Daleks were operated completely manually by the actors inside. But Mike Tucker and his team created a radio-controlled version of the head complete with controllable eye stalk and lights. This allowed actor

Barnaby Edwards to concentrate on the other aspects of Dalek movement, although a 'standard' head was also created as an emergency back-up.

As well as a new colour scheme and extra detailing and design refinements, a 'dog-tag' identification symbol was added under the eye – in effect a way for each Dalek to be identified.

Top: The Dalek construction crew – Scott Wayland, Mike Tucker, Nick Kool, Melvyn Friend.
Left (top): Scott Wayland and Nick Kool fix a new base to an existing 'body' section.
Left (middle): Nick Kool fixes slats to the exposed Dalek prop.
Left (bottom): Melvyn Friend fixes an eye-stalk shroud to a Dalek dome.
Above: The first full movement test for the almost complete, but unpainted, Dalek.

DALEK

Written by
Robert Shearman
Featuring
the Ninth Doctor and Rose
First broadcast
30 April 2005
1 episode

Rose has never before encountered a Dalek, but the Doctor has plenty of experience of their destructive capabilities. Will Rose and others heed the Doctor's warning? Or will they learn the hard way just how deadly the Daleks are?

Before long, the old battle cry rings out again in grating metallic tones: Exterminate! Exterminate! EXTERMINATE!

ROBERT SHEARMAN, WRITER

'When I was a kid, I was too scared to watch **Doctor Who**. It was my sister's fault, and the way she described the Daleks. They sounded terrifying! For years I was afraid even to put rubbish in the dustbins.

'Being asked to write for them was just as frightening. They're truly iconic – the ultimate monster, vindictive and brutish and spitting out laser bolts of hate. Their design is brilliant, losing the human shape so they seem wholly alien. But their characters are gleefully familiar – Daleks are everything we want to be when we're chidren, if we didn't have parents or teachers to get in our way!

'Bringing them back after over fifteen years off screen was a collaborative effort, and everyone wanted to emphasise that there's a real emotional creature inside that pepperpot casing – far more frightening than a bland robot. It was a great responsibility to take these monsters that were loved and feared by my generation, and make them loved and feared again. But it was tremendously satisfying.

'And, yes, I'm still scared of dustbins. My sister and the Daleks – they've both got a lot to answer for.'

Robert Shearman and 'friend'.

Above and opposite (left and right): The Dalek breaks free from its cell.

Right: The Dalek is held captive, chained in place.

Far right: The regenerated Dalek goes into battle.

SCRIPT EXTRACT - *DALEK*

```
AND OUT OF THE DARKNESS A TERRIBLE, RUSTING
VOICE. TWO SMALL LIGHTS BLINK IN UNISON WITH
THE WORDS...

DALEK
DOC... TOR...?

ON THE DOCTOR. SUDDEN, PROFOUND TERROR.
```

THE HAEMOVORES

If Fenric, the quintessence of evil, has his way then thousands of years in the future, *Homo sapiens* will evolve into Haemovores: creatures with an insatiable appetite for blood. Fenric's manipulation of time has enabled the Ancient One (see opposite) to travel back from a future Earth dying in the pollution of the post-industrial age, to infect people and turn them into Haemovores since Viking times.

Once infected, the victim becomes a pale vampire-like figure. But over time they mutate into hideous, grey-green creatures that can live in the sea. Their destiny is bound to the will of Fenric – they are his 'wolves' – and predicted by the legends of Norse mythology. The 'infection' has followed the journey of the flask in which Fenric is imprisoned and which was stolen by Viking raiders.

Discoloured skin with pustules and suckers, possibly developed underwater

Clawed, talon-like fingers

Faith can hold back a Haemovore – Russian Captain Sorin's faith in the Revolution; Ace's faith in the Doctor…

Clothing may be the best indication of the era when the victim was originally infected

FENRIC

Fenric is an elemental force of evil, born out of the creation of the universe itself. Seventeen hundred years ago, the Doctor carved bones from the desert sands into chess-pieces, and challenged Fenric to solve his puzzle. Fenric failed, and as a result was trapped in the Shadow Dimensions, within an ancient flask.

Fenric's 'wolves' have unwittingly worked to bring about Fenric's escape, and are descendants of Joseph Sundvik, a Viking who buried the flask. Once freed, Fenric first takes over the crippled body of Doctor Judson (above), and later that of the Russian Captain Sorin. The Doctor again sets Fenric a chess problem, which he cannot resist. The solution involves the white pawns turning on their own king – just as the Ancient One turns on Fenric.

The wolves of Fenric – Haemovores – return to do their leader's bidding.

THE CURSE OF FENRIC

The Doctor and Ace arrive at a secret military base during World War II. Here, Doctor Judson's 'Ultima Machine' decodes German ciphers, and Naval Commander Millington has discovered a source of poison beneath a local church, and plans to use it to attack Germany. Also buried there is an ancient flask, which contains the essence of Fenric – an elemental evil from the dawn of time, trapped by the Doctor centuries ago.

Fenric is released, and his Haemovores attack the base. The Doctor again challenges Fenric, who succeeds and prepares to send the Ancient One to poison the seas so that mankind will be replaced by Haemovores. But the Doctor persuades the Ancient One to destroy Fenric.

Written by
Ian Briggs
Featuring
the Seventh Doctor
and Ace
First broadcast
25 October 1989 –
15 November 1989
4 episodes

VAMPIRES

Jean and Phyllis have been evacuated from London during the Blitz, and become friends of Ace. Infected by a Haemovore while swimming in the sea, they mutate into vampire-like creatures.

They are destroyed by the Ancient One once Fenric has no further use for them, dissolving and rotting to dust.

THE ANCIENT ONE

The Ancient One, possibly called Ingiger, is the last living creature on a future Earth. Having watched the world die in the chemical waste, Ingiger was carried back by Fenric in a time storm to ninth-century Transylvania. Since only Fenric could return the creature to its own time, Ingiger sought the flask in which Fenric was trapped. A merchant bought the flask in Constantinople and Ingiger followed him through Europe, then pursued the Viking pirates who stole the flask.

Those it has killed and infected over the years have become Haemovores. But as it goes to spread the poison in the sea, the Ancient One kills the other Haemovores by thought. The Doctor manages to persuade Ingiger not to release the poison, but to kill Fenric instead.

THE ICE WARRIORS

The helmet includes sophisticated communications equipment

The Ice Warrior's voice is a strained hiss in Earth's atmosphere

A sonic disruptor, fitted on the upper wrist, can maim or kill

The huge Ice Warrior towers over humans

Tufts of fur emerge through joints in the armour

ICE LORDS

The Martian nobility, sometimes termed Ice Lords, are less heavily armoured, and have a more streamlined helmet. Higher ranks wear a ceremonial cloak and breastplate, which replaces the full armour of the lower classes. The ornamental belt suggests their 'skin' is a protective suit.

The Ice Warriors are originally from the planet Mars. As their name implies, they prefer a cold environment and are susceptible to heat. They are upright reptilian warriors, encased in shell-like armour so that very little of their actual bodies is visible – or vulnerable to attack. As a species, they have a long tradition of nobility and honour.

The Ice Warriors that the Doctor first encounters have been frozen for centuries beneath a glacier. The later Ice Warriors try to adapt Earth to suit their race and invade.

In the far future, they are friendly members of the Galactic Federation, though a group of them wants to return to the belligerent days of their past.

Victoria tries to escape from Turoc, an Ice Warrior.

THE ICE WARRIORS

An ice age grips the world of the future. At Britannicus Base, the Ioniser that holds back the glaciers is barely coping. The Doctor, Victoria and Jamie arrive and learn that an ancient warrior has been found in the glacier.

Revived, Varga (an Ice Warrior) kidnaps Victoria and awakens his crew. The humans, led by Clent, dare not use the Ioniser in case it causes the Martians' spaceship to explode and contaminate the area. The Ice Warriors, realising their world must be long dead, decide to make Earth theirs.

The Doctor gets control of the Ice Warriors' ship and its sonic weapons, making them retreat. Clent is forced to use the Ioniser as a weapon, stopping the glaciers and destroying Varga and his warriors.

Written by
Brian Hayles
Featuring
the Second Doctor, Jamie and Victoria
First broadcast
11 November 1967 –
16 December 1967
6 episodes

THE WARRIORS

The Ice Warriors are led by Varga, and his lieutenant, Zondal. There are three other warriors: Rintan, Isbur and Turoc. Knowing that the atmosphere of Mars is (or was) mainly nitrogen with almost no hydrogen or oxygen, the Doctor realises the Martians will choke on ammonium sulphide – as indeed Zondal does.

First and foremost the Martians are warriors. Varga is determined to triumph, and laughs at the strategic naivety of his opponents, a rasping, coughing sound. When thinking, or possibly sleeping, his head slumps inside his shell like a turtle.

SONIC WEAPONS

Each of the Warriors has a sonic weapon built in to their right forearm, which is fired by clenching the clamp-like fist. The main armament of the Martian ship is a sonic cannon, which also uses sound waves to destroy the objects in its path. When Zondal fires the sonic cannon at Britannicus Base, one entire wing of the house is destroyed.

THE ICE AGE

The carbon dioxide level in the Earth's atmosphere helps retain the sun's heat. The creation of artificial food means that most arable land has been built over, and plants reduced to an absolute minimum. The resulting lack of carbon dioxide has caused the new ice age.

Ionisation is a method of intensifying the sun's heat onto the Earth, into specific areas. But precise control is not easy. Ionisation can produce heat intense enough to melt rock.

Slaar – leader of the Ice Warriors who take over T-Mat Control on the moon.

THE SEEDS OF DEATH

Written by
Brian Hayles
Featuring
the Second Doctor,
Jamie and Zoe
First broadcast
25 January 1969 –
1 March 1969
6 episodes

T-Mat is a system for instantly transporting goods and people. Other forms of transport are now rarely used, and rockets have become obsolete. So when T-Mat Control on the moon stops working, the Doctor, Jamie and Zoe are sent in an illegal rocket to investigate.

The Ice Warriors have taken over, and plan to use Martian seed pods to sap oxygen from the Earth's atmosphere and make the planet like Mars. The Doctor realises that water will destroy the resulting fungus, but an Ice Warrior has been despatched to the Weather Control Station. The Doctor destroys the Warrior and makes it rain, before sabotaging the Martians' homing signal so that their fleet plunges into the sun.

THE WARRIORS

In overall charge of the invasion is the Grand Marshal. He is similar to the Ice Lord Slaar, who leads the raid on the moon. He speaks 'normally' as he is in his own atmosphere.

Some Ice Warriors are destroyed with a weapon built from a solar amplifier from the moon's solar-energy store. Focusing dishes attached to a solar power line from the solar amplifier seem to melt the Warriors away so that just a pool of fluid is left on the floor.

SEED PODS

The Martian seed pods are white spheres that grow and burst, releasing a mist of spores and killing anyone nearby through oxygen starvation.

The first developments of fungus are seen as vegetable blight. The large fungus bursts, spreading its spores. Acres of ground are covered in minutes and strong southwesterly winds could spread the disease from London over large parts of Europe, killing crops. The Doctor manages to destroy the fungus with torrential rain.

T-MAT

Travelmat Relay (T-Mat for short) is the ultimate form of travel. The control centre for the system is on the moon, serving receptions at all major cities on Earth. Travelmat provides an instantaneous means of public travel, sending raw materials and vital food supplies to all parts of the world.

While departure and arrival are from and to specific booths, the Ice Warriors have the controls reset so as to materialise the Doctor in space in order to kill him.

Alpha Centauri, Izlyr and the Doctor confront delegate Arcturus.

THE CURSE OF PELADON

The planet Peladon is being assessed for membership of the Galactic Federation. Delegates from member planets arrive, and the Doctor is mistaken for the Earth delegate. He is wary of the Martian delegate, Izlyr, and his sub-delegate, Ssorg, especially as the Chancellor of Peladon has been killed, apparently by the spirit of the royal beast, Aggedor.

But with Izlyr and Ssorg's help, the Doctor discovers that it is the High Priest Hepesh who wants to prevent Peladon joining the Federation. Hepesh has found an Aggedor creature, thought to be extinct, and trained it to obey him. The Doctor must defeat the King's Champion in single combat and tame Aggedor before he can avert the attempted coup.

Written by
Brian Hayles
Featuring
the Third Doctor
and Jo
First broadcast
29 January 1972 –
19 February 1972
4 episodes

THE FEDERATION

The Galactic Federation is a league of planets and civilisations governed by a shared charter, but retaining local customs and laws where appropriate – for example, for religious ceremonies.

Lord Izlyr is the delegate from Mars, which has presumably been repopulated. Izlyr says the Martians were once a race of warriors, but they now reject violence.

Alpha Centauri is a hermaphrodite hexapod with a high-pitched voice, one large eye and six arms. Arcturus resembles a large, tentacled head, kept in a mobile life-support system.

PELADON

Peladon is a pre-technological medieval planet. Young King Peladon, whose mother was from Earth, rules from the storm-swept Citadel of Peladon – a remote castle built into the side of a desolate mountain.

Hepesh is High Priest of Aggedor, Torbis is Chancellor. King Peladon calls them brothers but this may be a term of affection and common purpose rather than familial relationship. Hepesh fears that becoming a member of the Federation will mean that Peladon will be changed forever for the worse.

THE LEGEND OF AGGEDOR

The legend of the curse of Peladon concerns the royal beast of Peladon, now extinct. It is written: 'Mighty is Aggedor, fiercest of all the beasts of Peladon.' Young men would hunt it to prove their courage. Its fur trims the royal garment, its head is the royal emblem.

It is also written that there will come a day when the spirit of Aggedor will rise again to warn and defend his royal master, King Peladon. For at that day a stranger will appear in the land, bringing peril to Peladon and great tribulation to his kingdom.

Commander Azaxyr and Sarah have different ideas about the future of Peladon.

THE MONSTER OF PELADON

Written by
Brian Hayles
Featuring
the Third Doctor
and Sarah
First broadcast
23 March 1974 –
27 April 1974
6 episodes

Arriving on Peladon fifty years after his previous visit, the Doctor finds it again troubled. Queen Thalira is struggling to keep the trisilicate miners in order as the spirit of Aggedor is apparently angry with them. Alpha Centauri, Federation Ambassador, sends for security forces, and a group of Ice Warriors arrives led by Commander Azaxyr and his adjutant, Sskel.

But Azaxyr is acting on his own initiative, hoping to ship Peladon's valuable trisilicate to the Federation's enemies in Galaxy Five. The Doctor and Sarah manage to unite the court and the miners against the Ice Warriors and expose the technological trickery used to make Aggedor appear and kill the miners.

AZAXYR'S WARRIORS

Commander Azaxyr assumes control of Peladon when he arrives, imposing martial law. He leads a breakaway group of Martians who want to return to their former days of strength and conquest. Azaxyr has betrayed the Federation, but for military glory rather than material wealth. For the first time the Martians refer to themselves as Ice Warriors.

THE FEDERATION

The Federation is at war with Galaxy Five, which staged a vicious and unprovoked attack on them and now refuses to negotiate. Federation technology is based on the amber-like mineral trisilicate. Whoever controls a supply of trisilicate will win the war.

Eckersley is a Federation mining engineer from Earth. He is actually in league with Azaxyr and working for Galaxy Five. His Aggedor projection works by sending an image of the Aggedor statue with a matter projector while a directional heat ray kills miners.

Eckersley's innocent mining associate is one of the mole-like people of Vega – Vega Nexos. He has large eyes with small pupils, and a hair-covered face, legs and arms.

Bernard Bresslaw has his costume fitted as he assumes the role of Varga.

CREATING THE ICE WARRIORS

SCRIPT EXTRACTS –
THE ICE WARRIORS

INSIDE THE ICE,
DISTORTED BUT
RECOGNISABLE, IS
WHAT APPEARS TO
BE A HELMETED
WARRIOR. THE
HELMET IS
HOOD-LIKE AND
OMINOUS, IN THE
STYLE OF THAT
USED UNDER THE
OPENING TITLES OF
'HEREWARD THE
WAKE'.

THE MONSTER OF PELADON

THE MASSIVE DOOR
GRINDS OPEN
SLOWLY. ORTRON
AND THE GUARDS,
COMING UPON GEBEK
AND DOCTOR WHO,
STOP IN THEIR
TRACKS, STARING
AT THE OPEN DOOR-
WAY. STANDING IN
IT IS THE GRIM
FIGURE OF AN ICE
WARRIOR. IT
RAISES ITS MIGHTY
FIST, ON WHICH IS
SET ITS SONIC
EXTERMINATOR.

Writer Brian Hayles originally thought of his Ice Warriors as being closer to human soldiers in medieval-style space armour. It was costume designer Martin Baugh who hit on the idea of a reptilian biped fused into its armoured shell. His initial idea was for a kind of upright crocodile with a Viking-like helmet.

Once the designs were complete, the Ice Warrior suits were made, largely of fibreglass with rubber joints. Despite the joints, they were inflexible, and had to be bolted together with the actor inside. The mouth was made up with latex to appear reptilian. A plan to make the eyes glow behind the tinted glass covers was dropped, as the suits were quite hot enough without putting light bulbs inside them.

The director of *The Ice Warriors*, Derek Martinus, cast Bernard Bresslaw as Varga. He was a very tall actor, best known for his frequent appearances in the *Carry On* series of films. It was Bresslaw who created the distinctive voice of the Warriors. Thinking of how reptilian the costume looked, he experimented with a hissing, lizard-like voice. It was not treated, but because of the problems of acting and speaking in the full make-up and costume, the voices were pre-recorded then played back into the studio. The actors playing the Warriors then synched their lips to the recording. In *The Monster of Peladon*, the pre-recorded Warrior voices were not even spoken by the actors playing the Warriors. They were actually provided by **Doctor Who** producer (and former actor) Barry Letts.

The effect of the Ice Warriors' sonic disruptors was a visual distortion of the target as it is 'hit' by the sound waves. This was achieved by pointing the camera at a sheet of flexible mirrored plastic showing a reflection of the target. When the plastic was pushed gently from behind, so the image was distorted and wobbled.

THE MASTER

Like the Doctor, the Master is a renegade Time Lord. But unlike the Doctor, he is motivated by a lust for power and a love of chaos and destruction. The Doctor and the Master were apparently at school together and used to be friends. Certainly the Time Lords are aware of their former association as they initially warn the Doctor of the Master's arrival on Earth.

The Master is urbane, sophisticated and charming. His face – especially his eyes – hint at his terrible power. He can hypnotise the weak-minded with a few words, and destroy worlds on a whim. For his part, the Doctor pretends to be unimpressed, branding the Master 'an unimaginative plodder', but his respect for the Master is undeniable.

Far right: The original incarnation of the Master; Right: The Master in regenerated form; Above: The Master as he appears when the Eighth Doctor meets him.

MASTER PLANS

Terror of the Autons – The Master helps the Nestenes in their plan to invade Earth, but is defeated by the Third Doctor and UNIT.

The Mind of Evil – The Master uses a mind parasite in his bid to disrupt a peace conference and start a war.

The Claws of Axos – The Master brings an alien parasite, Axos, to Earth to drain all energy on the planet.

Colony in Space – Posing as an intergalactic adjudicator, the Master tries to find the deadly Doomsday Weapon on a distant planet.

The Daemons – The Master poses as a village vicar to do a deal with the devil-like creature Azal, last of the Daemons.

The Sea Devils – The Master helps the Sea Devils in their quest to reclaim Earth for themselves.

The Time Monster – The Master harnesses the ancient power of the Chronovores and causes the destruction of the city of Atlantis.

Frontier in Space – Working for the Daleks, the Master uses Ogrons to try to provoke a war between Earth and the Draconian Empire.

The Deadly Assassin – Dying at the end of his regenerative cycle, the emaciated Master returns to Gallifrey to trap the Fourth Doctor.

The Keeper of Traken – The Master gets a new body, at last.

Logopolis – The Master tries to learn the great secret of the city of Logopolis, and almost destroys the universe in the process.

Castrovalva – The Master sets a complex space–time trap for the newly regenerated Fifth Doctor, luring him to the strange city of Castrovalva.

Time-Flight – The Master hijacks a British Airways Concorde and brings it back to prehistoric Earth.

The King's Demons – In the thirteenth century, the Master uses a robot copy of King John to trick the Doctor.

The Five Doctors – The Master is sent to help the Doctor in the Death Zone on Gallifrey.

Planet of Fire – A miniaturised Master struggles to regain his full size and to bring about the Doctor's defeat.

The Mark of the Rani – The Master works with the Rani, another renegade Time Lord scientist, in nineteenth-century England.

The Trial of a Time Lord – The Master tries to take advantage of the Doctor's trial at the hands of the Time Lords.

Survival – The Master is trapped on an alien planet, mutating into a savage cheetah-like creature.

Doctor Who: The Movie – Although the Master has been executed by the Daleks, he is not dead. He takes over the body of a paramedic in San Francisco in 1999, but it is the Doctor's body he really wants.

The Fourth Doctor and Sarah encountered the Morbius Monster in a four-episode adventure called *The Brain of Morbius*, first shown in January 1976.

Before he rebelled, Morbius led the High Council of the Time Lords and 'dreamed the greatest dreams in history'. A war criminal with thousands of fanatical followers, he promised them the Elixir of Life. The Time Lords defeated Morbius's army on the planet Karn, and Morbius was executed.

But surgeon Mehendri Solon managed to rescue the brain of Morbius. On Karn, he constructed a new body for his hero, using bits and pieces from the remains of crashed space travellers. When the Doctor arrives on Karn, Solon realises that he has found his last donor and plans to use the Doctor's head. But the Doctor escapes, and Solon is forced to use a dangerous plastic brain-case to allow Morbius to live again.

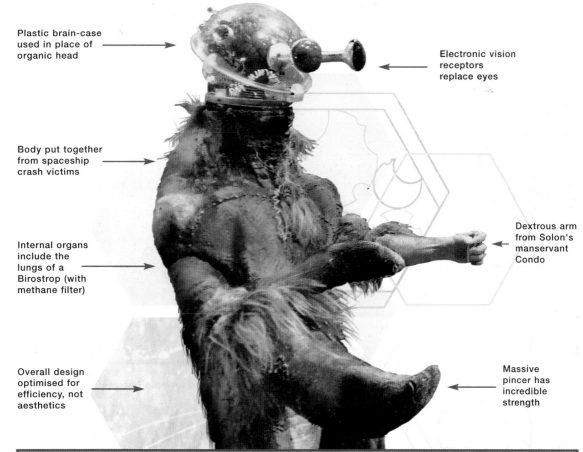

Plastic brain-case used in place of organic head

Electronic vision receptors replace eyes

Body put together from spaceship crash victims

Dextrous arm from Solon's manservant Condo

Internal organs include the lungs of a Birostrop (with methane filter)

Overall design optimised for efficiency, not aesthetics

Massive pincer has incredible strength

A NEW BODY

Solon (right) designed Morbius's new body for efficiency, not appearance. Hence, it has the lungs of a Birostrop, and the left arm of Solon's servant, Condo. The artificial brain-case is dangerous as static electricity can build up within the cranial cavity and may earth through the brain, upsetting its equilibrium and dislocating the neural centres.

Solon keeps the brain of Morbius suspended in a colloidal nutrient (left). Artificial vocal cords enable him to speak. Note that the brain is too large to fit inside the head of Condo or Sarah, so the Doctor is the only possible donor.

PLATFORM ONE: THE VISITORS

PLATFORM ONE

Five billion years in the future, Platform One floats above the Earth – a planet about to be destroyed as the sun expands and envelops it. Platform One is a sprawling, three-mile-wide space station.

From the Luxury Area, various life forms gather to watch the End of the World – Earthdeath – followed by drinks in the platform's Manchester Suite, a maximum hospitality zone. The guests are protected from the immense heat of the sun by copyrighted SunFilter Technology applied to all external surfaces and observation ports. Preserved for years by the National Trust, there is now no money to run the gravity satellites that have protected the deserted Earth from the fire of the sun.

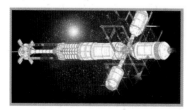

Top: Matthew Savage's concept painting of the Manchester Suite.

Above: The original design of Platform One.

THE STEWARD

Platform One is governed by the Steward, an ever-polite and diplomatic blue-skinned humanoid determined to ensure that Earthdeath goes to plan and that all his important guests are well catered for and at ease.

He is assisted by a staff of uniformed, diminutive blue-skinned humanoids who scurry about Platform One ensuring everything runs smoothly.

DESIGNING PLATFORM ONE

Platform One was created as a computer-generated image. But, as Matthew Savage's designs and concept paintings show, a great deal of thought was put into exactly how the space station would look and operate. The Manchester Suite is situated in the end section of the Platform – the main column of which can be seen rising above it in the illustration (right).

Right: A painting showing the position of the Manchester Suite.

Above: The final computer-generated image of Platform One.

PLATFORM ONE: THE VISITORS

THE END OF THE WORLD

Written by
Russell T Davies
Featuring
the Ninth Doctor
and Rose
First broadcast
2 April 2005
1 episode

The Doctor and Rose join the guests on Platform One to witness the end of planet Earth as it is burned away by the expanding sun, at a time five billion years in our future. But not all the guests visiting the Platform are there merely as sightseers – at least one of the group is a murderer.

With robotic spiders systematically sabotaging the Platform, and the number of deaths steadily rising, it is up to the Doctor and Rose to discover the truth and unmask the culprit. But whatever happens, can they survive the End of the World?

Top: Visitors and staff await the End of the World.

Above: The diminutive staff of Platform One.

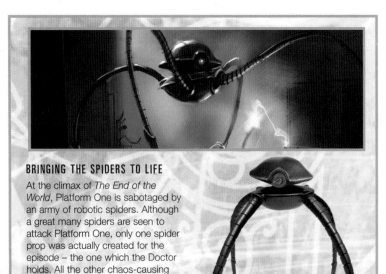

BRINGING THE SPIDERS TO LIFE

At the climax of *The End of the World*, Platform One is sabotaged by an army of robotic spiders. Although a great many spiders are seen to attack Platform One, only one spider prop was actually created for the episode – the one which the Doctor holds. All the other chaos-causing spiders were computer-generated images, added to the story in post-production. The spider was designed by Alex Fort.

THE ADHERENTS OF THE REPEATED MEME

The Adherents of the Repeated Meme are apparently from Financial Family Seven. They recite their 'meme' at thirty-minute intervals, in their whispering graveyard voices. Little or nothing of their features can be seen under their hooded cloaks, except for their part-metal, part-organic claws. And as the Doctor discovers, the Adherents are not all that they seem...

SCRIPT EXTRACT –
THE END OF THE WORLD

Five cowled monk-like figures, faces hooded in darkness, like the Ghost of Christmas Future crossed with a Dementor. A sinister hum follows them round.

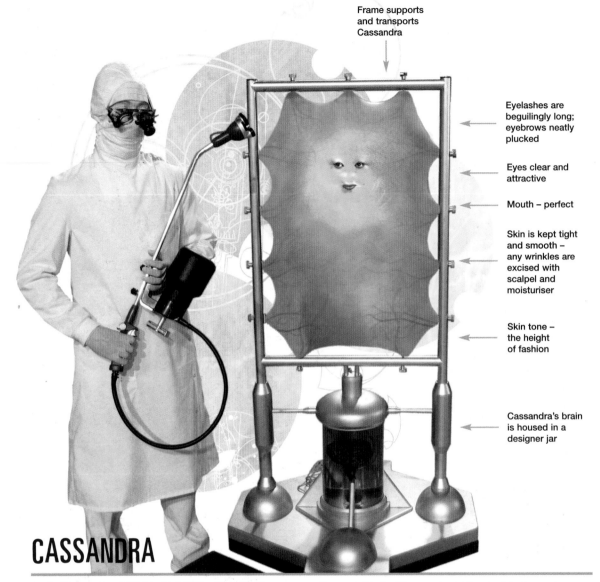

Frame supports and transports Cassandra

Eyelashes are beguilingly long; eyebrows neatly plucked

Eyes clear and attractive

Mouth – perfect

Skin is kept tight and smooth – any wrinkles are excised with scalpel and moisturiser

Skin tone – the height of fashion

Cassandra's brain is housed in a designer jar

CASSANDRA

Lady Cassandra O'Brien Dot Delta Seventeen considers herself to be the last human – her father was Texan and her mother from the Arctic Desert. They were born and were buried on Earth. Other humans have survived, of course, but mingled and crossbred with other life forms. Cassandra considers herself to be 'pure'.

But after years of enhancement and cosmetic surgery, and genetic (and gender) manipulation (708 operations in all), Cassandra is now a thin piece of skin stretched across a metal frame – all that remains of her face. As soon as any wrinkles appear, she has them cut out with a scalpel. The mobile frame is as tall and wide as a man, and Cassandra's brain resides in a nutrient tank at its base.

Attended at all times by her personal surgeons, Cassandra has recently had her chin taken in, so as to be even more flat. She prides herself on not looking a day over two thousand and moisturises constantly. She has been married several times.

As gifts, Cassandra brings to Platform One the last ever ostrich egg (the birds became extinct in 2051), and what she believes is an I-Pod – though this is, in fact, a 1950s jukebox.

LIVES OF THE RICH AND THIN

An extract from Vox B. MacMallican's best seller, translated by Russell T Davies.

Many have tried to write a biography of the Lady Cassandra O'Brien Dot Delta Seventeen, and many have died mysteriously in the process. She has guarded the secrets of her past with lawyers, bile and the occasional dagger. This much we know: she was born as Brian Edward Cobbs, in the ruins of the Walsall Apology, in the Old Calendar Year of 4.99/4763/A/15.

Cassandra often made outlandish claims about her parentage. Stories of lords and ladies and Eskimos would seem to be blatant lies; certainly, her title was a complete invention – the Dot Delta Seventeens appear nowhere in *Burke's Extrapolated*, and there is evidence that the 'Lady' was purchased for 50 klim at the Instant Royalty Bazaar.

Not much is known about her early years. There is evidence of a Mr B. E. Cobbs, registered as a security guard at Klime Enterprises in the OC Year A/32. Two years later, a Miss B. E. Cobbs marries Harry Klime, the billionaire owner of the company. Six months later, Harry Klime is found dead, having fallen on his own garden rake, five times. Mrs Cobbs-Klime inherited the empire, but when police called in a rake expert, she cashed in her shares and promptly vanished.

In the OC Year A/60, a thumbprint matching that of Mrs Cobbs-Klime was found on the body of a murdered punter at the Linkladen Bordello, on the lawless border world of Rit. The bordello's madam, a lady going by the name of Kitty Gillespie, vanished that night and was last seen boarding the shuttle to Sant's World.

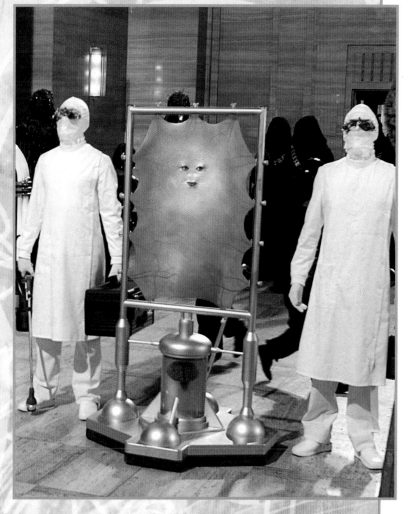

And it's here, on Sant's World, twenty years later, that we find the first record of a woman operating under the name Cassandra. First, an actress by the name of Cassandra Hoots appears in B-movie gems such as *Mind My Legs* and *Run, Betty, Run*. This woman marries the studio boss, Ivor Cannabone, and after Ivor's death beneath a falling piano, Mrs Cannabone becomes head of the company. In this year, the original Brian Cobbs suddenly resurfaces, as the star of the musical biopic *Look At Me Laughing!* The reviews are terrible, fifteen critics and two surgeons mysteriously die, and Brian is never heard of again.

In the OC Year B/01, Cannabone Pictures collapses, but Cassandra flees the planet, travelling in steerage (perhaps this is what prompted her later collection of poems, *Forlorn and Lonely, Sitting on a Box of Chickens*). But soon she's seen on the arm of royalty, consorting with the one-thousand-year-old Prince Regent Lucius at the Fifteenth Pylomic Games. Marriage swiftly follows. Of course, a terrible gliding accident soon befalls the entire Lucius family, leaving Princess Cassandra as the only living heir, but now, for the first time, I can exclusively reveal, that this was no –

(These were the last words written by Vox B. MacMallican, before her sudden and mysterious death by fountain pen.)

MAKING-UP CASSANDRA

Cassandra was a challenge for the production team to create. Right from the start it was apparent that Cassandra's face would have to be a computer-generated image, and her voice would need to be added in post-production. However, a prop was needed for the actors to relate to, and she had to respond and speak in real time during filming.

So a 'stunt' Cassandra was built – a static face that the other actors could react to and 'play off'. This was removed for some sequences, and the empty frame prop used, so that the computer-generated face could be added cleanly later.

As well as a 'stunt' face, Cassandra had a voice double. Actress Clare Cage spoke Cassandra's lines off-stage during recording. Clare's voice was then removed when Cassandra's 'real' voice – that of noted actress Zoë Wanamaker – was added.

SCRIPT EXTRACT - *THE END OF THE WORLD*

```
CASSANDRA glides in.
A metal frame, six feet tall, three feet
wide. Only an inch deep. And stretched
across the frame, a piece of canvas -
bolted into the frame, pulled tight.
Except this isn't canvas. It's skin.
Right in the middle, there are two eyes
and a mouth. No nose, no chin, nothing
but eyes and mouth. The eyes are bulging,
but the mouth has no depth; it's just
lips and teeth, no actual mouth behind
it. When the lips are open you can see
right through. The whole frame is
supported on a sleek metal truck. At the
base, in a glass jar, a brain bubbles and
glows from within, wires connecting it to
the frame.

CASSANDRA
Moisturise me.
```

Top left: The Cassandra prop with the face removed for CGI.
Top right: The first concept sketch was drawn by Russell T Davies.
Above: The Cassandra prop, complete with 'static' face.

THE FACE OF BOE

From the Silver Devastation, the Face of Boe is the official sponsor for the festivities surrounding the End of the World. The Face itself is held in a fluid-filled life-support tank powered by antiquated, steam-driven technology.

Above and left: The Face of Boe witnesses the End of the World in the Manchester Suite on Platform One.

LEGENDS OF THE UNIVERSE

By J. B. Dane. An extract from the Stellar Edition, translated from the original hieromanx by Russell T Davies.

It is said that the Face of Boe has lived forever. Certainly, there is evidence that he was present when the stars of Andromeda were still nothing but dust. And his presence, billions of years later, at the End of the Earth, is on public record.

No one knows if the Face of Boe can die; perhaps not even the Face himself. His longevity is a mystery; it is not due to the gases of his tank, nor the coils of his DNA. It is as if he lives by will alone. Or by mistake. On the integrated planets of Cep Cassalon, the Face is known as 'the Creature that God Forgot'.

He has borne children; he was particularly fertile during the Fourth Great and Bountiful Human Empire, carrying three sons and three daughters. But all six Boemina lived a natural life span of forty years and no more. The Face of Boe watched his children die, and stayed watching while the world forgot they had even existed.

Legend has it that if the Face of Boe should die one day, then the sky will crack asunder. And it is said that he holds one, final secret; that he will speak this secret, with his final breath, to one person and one person alone. A homeless, wandering traveller…

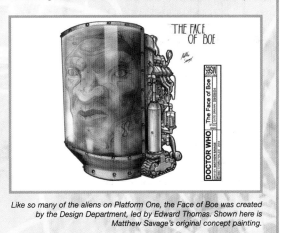

THE FACE OF BOE

DOCTOR WHO   The Face of Boe

Like so many of the aliens on Platform One, the Face of Boe was created by the Design Department, led by Edward Thomas. Shown here is Matthew Savage's original concept painting.

THE FOREST OF CHEEM

Bark instead of skin

Heads sprout shoots and leaves

Humanoid features, but grown from wood

Wooden hands are very dextrous

SCRIPT EXTRACT – *THE END OF THE WORLD*

The FOREST walks in. Three humanoid figures in white robes, but with bark for skin. Their 'hair' is a series of thin branches, with the occasional leaf, twined back like wicker.

The Forest of Cheem is a collective of 'Trees' – humanoid creatures grown from wood, sprouting branches and leaves. Jabe, Lute and Coffa represent the Forest on Platform One for the viewing of the End of the World.

It is traditional for the Trees of the Forest to offer cuttings from their relatives as peace-offerings and gifts. The more revered and illustrious the relative, the greater the value of the gift.

They do not respect or understand technology – Jabe refers to the mainframe that controls Platform One as 'the metalmind' and her own personal digital assistant as a 'metalmachine'.

The Trees have massive forests on many planets – making them rich as investors in land. Earth is important to them as so many of their species evolved from trees from Earth. Jabe, for example, is a direct descendant of the tropical rainforest.

FROM THE PLATFORM ONE GUEST LIST

Information about each of the guests invited to witness the End of the World was given to the Steward. Reproduced here is the information about visitor Jabe and the Forest of Cheem. Extract translated by Russell T Davies.

The origins of the Forest of Cheem go all the way back to the Middle Blue Period of the Planet Earth. In the Fifth Calendar Year of 111222/9967, an area of land across the equator, approximately 500 miles long and 3 miles wide, was sold at auction, to alleviate the Earth's terrible debts. But while other victims of this illegal auction suffered terribly – Brazil and its five billion occupants were sold to the Deathsmiths of Goth, there to be experimented upon in bizarre and terrible ways – the Equatorial Patch was bought by the wise and wonderful Brothers of Hame. The Brotherhood, descendants of the legendary Halldons, consisted of genetic experts, dedicated to enhancing the universe with new forms of life. The Equatorial Patch was isolated on the Panjassic Asteroid Field, cultivated, fostered, nurtured, and its evolution accelerated.

The evolutionary journey of a billion years was thus compressed into a mere three hundred. First, the rainforest achieved a level-three sentience. Within two generations, the first treeforms were beginning to take shape, moulded in the bark, with arms reaching from treetops. It is written that: 'The wind in the branches became a single, harmonious voice.' Twenty years later, having been cradled in wombs of vine and sap, the treeforms were walking. Language and community and compassion came soon after.

Two hundred years after the start of the experiment, the Forest had named itself, taking the title Cheem from its word for water. It existed on the groves of the Asteroid Field as a separate theocracy, and soon resented the control of the ever-watchful Brotherhood. Minor skirmishes broke out when the Forest tried to assert its own evolutionary rights, and demanded an end to the Brotherhood's experiments. But the Brotherhood had learnt from early mistakes in genetic acceleration, and soon granted the forest complete independence.

Then, the path of the Forest takes a shadowy turn, the stuff of mythology. It is said that, as one, every treeform heard the Great Calling. The entire race boarded their barkships and fled the Asteroid Field, in the course of one night. They travelled to the far edges of the universe, and out of recorded history. What they saw there, what they learnt, is never spoken of. Some say the Forest met God; some say the Forest killed God; some say the Forest is God. But no treeform will ever discuss the Great Calling, its origin or its consequences. Nevertheless, the Forest returned from the depths of space, after an absence of five thousand years, with a wisdom and grace unparalleled in Fit Five civilisations. They have ascended to join the Higher Species. It is said that treeforms now walk in the most hallowed of halls. And while legends persist of a mighty, invisible Time War, it is said that the Forest alone observed the secret battle, and wept.

Now, as humanity's seed dissipates, and the Forest of Cheem's roots spread to all civilised worlds, the treeforms are treated with reverence, wherever they go.

Selected from the Forest's younger branches, out of the Caven Hol Arboretum, the Treeform Jabe Ceth Ceth Jafe is boarding Platform One to represent her species at the End of the World. The Corporation owning all Platforms and Associated Venues would like to welcome Jabe and her consorts, and hopes that she has an unforgettable, life-changing experience.

Left: Visitor Jabe of the Forest of Cheem.
Top: The result of super-evolving a tree.

THE MOXX OF BALHOON

The Moxx of Balhoon is a diminutive blue-skinned creature, supported by and transported on an anti-gravity chair. He represents the solicitors Jolco and Jolco. His speech is terse and to the point.

The Moxx has a short snout and sharp teeth.

Saliva may be projected from mouth in formal spitting

Legs not strong enough to support full weight of body

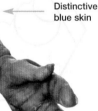

Distinctive blue skin

SAFETY PROCEDURES INVOLVING ANY CITH, MOXX OR GRAME OF BALHOON
Legislated by Russell T Davies.

The Moxx is part of the Rack Fen Jackovittie Rab Mol Mol 'feh' Mol Tassic Conglomerate, part of the Hanamacat Pel Jadrabone, part-associated with the Raccidane Hoblomeer, but independent of the Roc Maff Payteen Six. Genetic Code Registration 5.6.9.222.0.

The Moxx is blue. He travels on an anti-gravity chair. His accepted form of formal greeting is to spit. In an emergency, if his bodily fluids are not replaced by the chair's internal filter every 25 minutes, then the Moxx has been known to sweat glaxic acid. In this case, do not touch the Moxx. He will be grateful if you point out the problem. He might even reward you with coins of solid blick. Or perhaps a song. His favourite song is 'Yap Cap Forward Bigga Toom Toom Toom'.

Right: The Moxx and some of the other aliens created for The End of the World.

Below: Matthew Savage's design for the Moxx.

Bottom right: The Moxx on his anti-gravity chair, which contains an internal filter to replace essential bodily fluids.

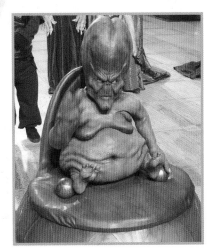

CREATING THE MOXX

It was originally planned that the Moxx of Balhoon would be a totally non-humanoid character created by computer animation. But as the planning for *The End of the World* progressed, the decision was taken to make the Moxx a more tangible character, played by an actor in heavy make-up. Designs for the Moxx were then created by Matthew Savage (see left) and realised by Neill Gorton, working for Edward Thomas, production designer.

As well as the mask and make-up, actor Jimmy Vee had artificial legs and feet stuck to his stomach. His own legs extended beneath the Moxx's chair – allowing him to push it along on castors.

Writer Russell T Davies originally envisaged the Moxx like this: 'The Moxx is a bowl of blue fat, piled high, with tiny black eyes. His bowl levitates six inches off the ground.'

Invited guests gather on Platform One to witness the End of the World.

AN INVITATION TO THE END OF THE WORLD

To swell the number of guests on Platform One, the **Doctor Who** design teams created several 'extra' aliens to appear in the background of crowd scenes in the Manchester Suite. Introductions to these aliens were added back into the script after they had been designed.

Although created for just a day's shooting, the pictures on these pages show the care and attention to detail that went into even the smallest part of the new series of **Doctor Who**.

Above: The Ambassadors from the city state of Binding Light.

Right: The brothers Hop Pyleen.

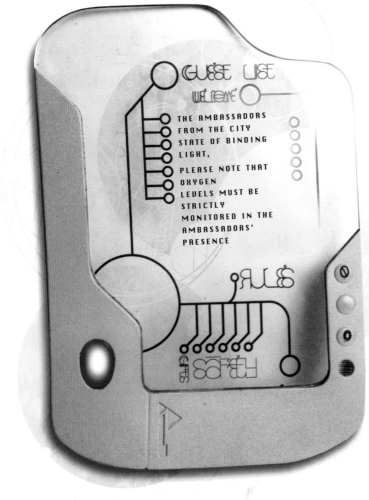

THE AMBASSADORS
FROM THE CITY
STATE OF BINDING
LIGHT,

PLEASE NOTE THAT
OXYGEN
LEVELS MUST BE
STRICTLY
MONITORED IN THE
AMBASSADORS'
PRESENCE

OTHER INVITED GUESTS INCLUDE...

From the exalted clifftops of Rex Vox Jax, the inventors and copyright holders of hyposlip travel systems, the Brothers Hop Pyleen

Cybernetic hyperstar Cal 'Spark Plug' MacNannovich and his entourage

Mr and Mrs Pakoo

Chosen scholars of Class Fifty-Five from the University of Rago Rago Five Six Rago

Above: Cybernetic hyperstar Cal 'Spark Plug' MacNannovich (right) and guest.

Right: Mr and Mrs Pakoo.

THE SILURIANS AND THE SEA DEVILS

Millions of years ago, the Earth was inhabited by intelligent reptiles. But when a small planet was detected approaching Earth, they thought it would draw away the atmosphere and create a global catastrophe. To avoid extinction, they built huge hibernation chambers, where they slept through the crisis. They would be awakened when the atmosphere returned.

But the small planet never drew away the Earth's atmosphere, and so the reptiles never woke. Instead the planet was captured by Earth's gravity and became the moon. The various groups of reptiles that have awoken since – called Silurians and Sea Devils by the people who first encountered them – regard the Earth as their planet, and humans as upstart apes to be destroyed.

Third eye can stun or kill. It can operate Silurian devices, and burn through rock

Weapon emits a charge that can burn through rock or metal

Amphibious Sea Devil can live underwater or on land

Unlike other reptiles, Silurians and Sea Devils walk upright

Combined snout and mouth

Scaly reptilian skin

EVOLVING TO SURVIVE

In *Warriors of the Deep* both Sea Devils and Silurians have changed. The Sea Devils now wear samurai-style body armour, while the Silurians have 'shells' protecting their torso. The Silurians' third eye illuminates when they speak, rather than – as in *The Silurians* – when they focus their mental energies.

The Doctor and the Brigadier do not see eye to eye in The Silurians.

THE SILURIANS

The Doctor and UNIT investigate mysterious power failures at a research centre on Wenley Moor. They discover that a nearby colony of Silurians is drawing off the power to revive more Silurians, who plan to wipe out mankind with a deadly plague. The Doctor manages to find a cure for the disease, but the Silurians take over the research centre and prepare to destroy the Van Allen belt, which shields Earth from the harmful radiation of the sun. If they were to succeed, humankind would die, but reptiles would thrive. The Doctor defeats the Silurians, who retire into hibernation, believing that the centre's reactor is about to explode. Against the Doctor's wishes the Brigadier destroys the Silurian base.

Written by
Malcolm Hulke
Featuring
the Third Doctor,
UNIT and Liz
First broadcast
31 January 1970 –
14 March 1970
7 episodes

MONSTER PET

The Silurians are able to control their pet dinosaurs using a signalling device that emits a high-pitched warble. This device can also be used to summon other Silurians. The first contact with the Silurians occurs when two cavers are attacked by the dinosaur, which is then called off by the Silurians. One of the men is killed, the other – Spencer – degenerates into a nervous condition brought on by the shock. Delirious, he draws on the sickbay wall – his pictures are similar to ancient cave paintings, but include images of Silurians.

THE PLAGUE

When primitive apes used to raid the Silurians' crops, they killed them with a poison. The Silurians release this poison to create a plague that will wipe out the human race – descendants of those apes.

Once infected, the victim develops pustules, then their skin becomes discoloured. Finally, they fall unconscious and die. The Silurians are sure the humans are too primitive to develop a cure – and they are right as it's the Doctor who finds a solution.

THE SEA DEVILS

Written by
Malcolm Hulke
Featuring
the Third Doctor
and Jo
First broadcast
26 February 1972 –
1 April 1972
6 episodes

When the Doctor and Jo visit the Master in his island prison, they find that ships have disappeared mysteriously in the area. Visiting the nearby naval base, the Doctor examines a charred lifeboat and concludes that the problem centres on an abandoned sea fort. Here, they encounter a Sea Devil. The navy submarine sent to investigate fails to return.

The Master has made contact with the Sea Devils, encouraging them to take over the naval base. He intends to help them reawaken the sleeping reptiles all over the world. But the Doctor booby-traps the Master's reactivation device. The two Time Lords escape from the Sea Devil base in the captured submarine moments before the device explodes.

HMS SEASPITE

The naval base, HMS Seaspite, is commanded by Captain John Hart. He is in charge of the adaptation of the sea fort for use as a SONAR testing station. The submarine, under Commander Ridgeway, is fitted with experimental SONAR equipment, which Hart hopes will detect the Sea Devils.

Other equipment that Captain Hart calls in to help deal with the Sea Devils includes an air-sea rescue helicopter, a hovercraft, a diving vessel, and a task force of naval vessels that depth-charge the Sea Devil base.

THE MASTER'S IMPRISONMENT

Captured by UNIT, the Master has been imprisoned indefinitely. There were calls for him to be executed, but the Doctor pleaded for clemency and now the Master is the only prisoner in a castle on an isolated island. The prison is patrolled by armed guards and protected by CCTV and minefields.

The prison's governor is Colonel Trenchard, a weak-minded man who has fallen under the Time Lord's influence. Under the Master's direction, Sea Devils take over the prison – releasing the Master and killing Trenchard.

Left: The revived Silurians make their plans.

Opposite: The Sea Devils believe the Earth belongs to them.

WARRIORS OF THE DEEP

The Doctor, Tegan and Turlough arrive in the underwater Seabase Four in 2084. The world is divided into two belligerent power blocs and the base is on constant alert – always ready to fire its deadly proton missiles.

But a group of Silurians and Sea Devils attack the base. Using a deadly, bio-engineered underwater creature called a Myrka, they gain control of the base and prepare to launch the missiles. They plan to provoke a war that will wipe out humanity, but leave the Earth undamaged for them to take over. By linking directly to the base weapons systems, the Doctor is able to stop the launch. The Silurians and Sea Devils are killed with hexachromite gas, which is deadly to reptiles.

Written by
Johnny Byrne
Featuring
the Fifth Doctor,
Tegan and Turlough
First broadcast
5 January 1984 –
13 January 1984
4 episodes

SEABASE FOUR

Seabase Four is one of several undersea bases that both power blocs use to monitor each other and detect and respond to any aggression. The base is heavily armed with proton missiles, which wipe out human life while leaving the environment relatively undamaged.

To eliminate any danger of computer error, missile-launch is controlled by a specially conditioned human whose mind can interface with the weapons system. But Seabase Four has been infiltrated by enemy agents, who have their own ideas about launching the missiles.

THE MYRKA

The Myrka is a large reptile with stubby forearms, bred by the Silurians as a living weapon. It is a bio-engineered creature capable of electrifying its victims simply by touching them.

But, unused to light since it lives in the depths of the ocean, it can be destroyed by exposure to certain wavelengths of light. The Doctor kills it with an ultra-violet converter.

The complicated Myrka costume is prepared for its appearance.

THE SLITHEEN

From the planet Raxacoricofallapatorius, the huge Slitheen are a family dedicated to business. They have long, hyphenated names. With their fine sense of smell, they hunt ritually, enjoying the chase.

Seeing the potential Earth offers as a commodity, once purged of its population and reduced to a radioactive energy source, they determine to stage a hostile takeover.

The Slitheen are composed of living calcium. Although they are over eight feet tall, they have the technology to compress their bodies and disguise themselves as humans.

Superb sense of smell aids hunting

Compression field control – can shrink Slitheen down to fit inside human disguise, but results in excess gas being produced

Massive strength – claw can lift a human easily

Endangered female Slitheen can fire a poison dart from her claw

Enormous Slitheen have to 'compress' to imitate humans

Creatures are composed of living calcium

DISGUISE

The Slitheen use advanced technology to squeeze themselves into body-suit disguises. In their attack on Earth they take the place of high-ranking British politicians to seize control.

Any large human could be a disguised Slitheen.

INFILTRATION!

To disguise themselves as humans, the Slitheen squeeze into artificial human body suits, sealed with a hidden zip across the forehead. They use a compression field – controlled by a device worn around the neck – to make their bodies fit inside the suits. Being so large, they can only shrink down far enough to impersonate very large people.

As a side effect of the compression field, gas is released – meaning that the disguised Slitheen have to make embarrassing bodily noises in order to vent it. The gas, caused by calcium decay, smells of bad breath. When the suit is opened, pent-up energy is released with electrical flashes round the zip and blue electrical discharges from the body suit.

Left: Margaret Blaine reveals her true identity.

Far left: A Slitheen emerges from its human disguise.

Certain members of the British Cabinet are not what they seem.

ALIENS OF LONDON and WORLD WAR THREE

Written by
Russell T Davies
Featuring
the Ninth Doctor
and Rose
First broadcast
16 April 2005 –
23 April 2005
2 episodes

The Doctor returns Rose to Earth just in time to witness a spaceship crash into the Thames. The press reports that First Contact has been made with an alien race – a body is found in the wreckage.

But as experts gather at Downing Street, and the Prime Minister disappears, the Doctor begins to suspect that not all is as it seems. Has there really been a crash-landing? Or is this all part of a dastardly ploy by aliens who are already on Earth, and whose plans for the planet are nearing completion? Trapped in the Cabinet Office, the Doctor and Rose together with Harriet Jones (MP for Flydale North) must decide whether to risk everything in a last-ditch bid to save the Earth.

Above: Crisis at Downing Street.

Right: A Slitheen attacks.

Left: Experts on alien incursion gather at Downing Street.

Below: The Doctor fights back.

Bottom left: The Doctor and Rose arrive at Number 10.

Bottom right: Slitheen outside the Cabinet Office.

THE ALIENS ARE HERE!

A spaceship crash-landing in the River Thames after colliding with the clock tower that houses Big Ben at the Palace of Westminster seems to signal the arrival of aliens on Earth. As the Doctor points out to Rose, the crash-landing is perfect – from the angle of descent to the colour of the trailing smoke.

But as he soon realises – it is too perfect. The crash has been staged by the Slitheen to draw attention away from their ship in the North Sea and to lure the world's experts on extraterrestrial incursion to London.

CRASH-LANDING

The effect of the spaceship crash-landing was achieved by a combination of live-action sequences, model work and CGIs. The Slitheen ship was designed by Bryan Hitch, and created at MillTV, while Mike Tucker was responsible for the large model of Big Ben and its destruction.

Above and left: Bryan Hitch's concept paintings of the Slitheen ship and (inset) the Slitheen ship crash-lands in the Thames.

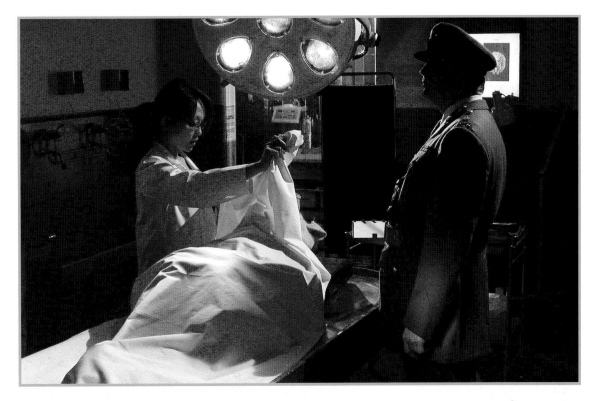

PIGS IN SPACE

As part of their deception, the Slitheen create a fake alien life form out of an ordinary farmyard pig. They dress it in a spacesuit and leave it to be found in the crashed ship.

The pig is taken to Albion Hospital, where it is examined by Doctor Sato. The pig has been augmented with Slitheen technology – it stands on its hind legs, and its brain has been 'wired up' and had components added to convince Doctor Sato that it is no hoax.

Despite the Doctor's attempts to befriend it, the terrified pig is shot by soldiers guarding the hospital.

Above: Doctor Sato and General Asquith examine a 'space alien'.

Right: Rather than use a real pig, the production team designed and built a pig costume, complete with spacesuit, which was worn by actor Jimmy Vee (who also played the Moxx of Balhoon – see page 67).

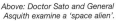

THE SLITHEEN TAKE SHAPE

The Slitheen were the first major new monsters designed for the 2005 series of **Doctor Who**. Along with the first episode, *Rose* (see page 10) – which featured the return of the Autons – the two-part *Aliens of London* story was one of the first into production, with some earlier episodes (including *The End of the World*, see page 58) being made later.

For the Slitheen, the designers, led by production designer Edward Thomas and concept artist Bryan Hitch, started with sketches and drawings inspired by the description scripted by Russell T Davies (see opposite). Dan Walker and Neill Gorton then created a model from which the final creatures were made. The costumes were made largely from latex, and were extremely bulky. They were also very heavy and hot for the actors to wear – especially as filming took place during a heat wave.

Top: Bryan Hitch's original designs for the Slitheen.

Middle left: A maquette – a small model – shows how the Slitheen will look.

Above: A Slitheen costume being assembled.

Right: The actors revealed inside the costumes.

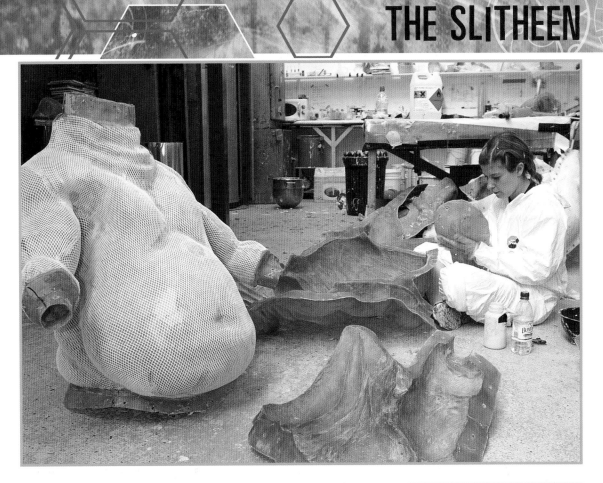

SCRIPT EXTRACT - *ALIENS OF LONDON*

IT'S EIGHT FEET TALL, A THICK TUBE OF SOLID,
WET, GREEN FLESH, ALL BRISTLING WITH SPIKES
AND SPINES. THE WHOLE THING CURVES OVER AT
THE TOP, LIKE AN UPRIGHT PRAWN, SO ITS HEAD
LEERS DOWN. A FACE LIKE A BIG, SWEET, BLOAT-
ED GREEN BABY, WITH JET-BLACK EYES. GREEN
SLIME TRICKLING FROM ITS TERRIBLE SMILE.

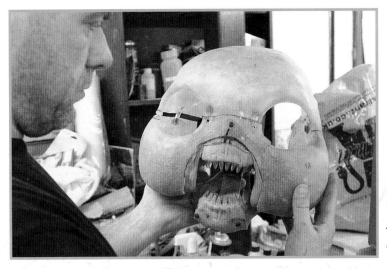

Top: Parts of the Slitheen suit are cast in latex.

Above: Another of Bryan Hitch's early drawings.

Left: A Slitheen head takes shape.

THE SLITHEEN

COMPUTING ALIENS

For some sequences, having an actor in a Slitheen costume was not practical. In particular, the suits were not designed for rapid movement – the heads 'waggled' if the actor inside tried to run. So the various chases through 10 Downing Street in *World War Three* had to be carefully planned.

Sometimes clever editing and rapid intercutting made it appear that Slitheen were hurrying through the corridors when in fact they were hardly moving. On other occasions computer-generated Slitheen were added to 'clean' images of the background and animated to show the creatures moving at speed.

Another complicated sequence was the Slitheen shedding of their human guise. Rather than having an actor in a Slitheen costume inside a human costume, the actor wore an all-over body suit marked with black crosses to give reference points to the animators. The actors inside the 'human suits' were then replaced in post-production with computer-generated Slitheen apparently squeezing out of their human guise.

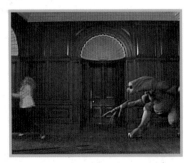

Above: A computer-animated Slitheen chases Rose through 10 Downing Street.

Right: Compare this CGI of a Slitheen with the actual costume on page 83.

RAXACORICOFALLAPATORIUS

Extract from *Jane's Book of Planets*, translated by Russell T Davies.

The world of Raxacoricofallapatorius is a beautiful place. Wild and yet graceful poppito trees blow in the cinnamon breeze; white marble temples sit atop cliffs of sapphire and chalk; endless burgundy oceans crash around spectacular ice-caves at the four poles.

The indigenous species, the Raxacoricofallapatorians, are civilised, elegant and proud. With skins of living calcium, and the wonders of slipstream compression technology at their disposal, they have a strict code of government, which educates their children in the disciplines of poetry, mathematics and democracy, from the day they are hatched.

Of course, every paradise has its serpent. The shame of Raxacoricofallapatorius is the Family Slitheen, descendants of the original Huspick Degenerate, cousins to the Blathereen and Rackateen, born far away from the main planetary continent on the Islands of Hisp. Over many centuries, the Slitheen established themselves as a criminal clan, infiltrating all levels of government, and subtly controlling the planet's off-world distribution of the valuable spice, Offich. They became so deeply embedded in government they threatened to tarnish their entire species with their crimes.

But in the Great Purge of Yon:556, the Slitheen were exposed, shamed, and arrested en masse. Many fled their homeworld. The entire clan – every cousin, step-sister, half-mother and fiancée – thought to number more than 550, was tried and found guilty, in perpetuity. Justice is harsh on Raxacoricofallapatorius. The surviving Slitheen have been given the death sentence in their absence, with no chance of appeal. Should a Slitheen ever return to the homeworld, they would be taken to the largest clifftop temple, the Palace of Enforced Atonement. There, a thin solution of acetic acid would be prepared. Watched by thousands of spectators in the open-air amphitheatre, all chanting the Dawn Prayer 'Oh Deliver Us Weeping And Shamed', the Slitheen would be lowered into the cauldron, slowly, and boiled. The solution would be tempered so that only the outer skin dissolves; the inside of the Slitheen would fall into the solution, to become soup. And for fifteen to twenty seconds, it is thought that the Slitheen would still be alive. A living soup. The resulting liquid would then be drunk by the priests and ministers of Raxas Prime.

To date, not one Slitheen has yet returned home.

Deprived of a homeworld, it is said that the Family has degenerated still further. Early attempts to make profits out of drug-running, arms-dealing and chizzle-waxing were thwarted by the local star-system's police force, the Wrarth Warriors. Scattered across the off-world archipelagos, and with their bank accounts frozen, the Slitheen have had to resort to ever more desperate measures to make money. But they have declared that they will survive, and return home one day. No matter what the cost.

THE SONTARANS

The Sontarans are a militaristic race dedicated to warfare. They have been at war with the Rutans for millennia, neither side gaining a lasting advantage in the struggle. From a high-gravity planet, the

Sontarans are a strong, stocky race, cloned at a rate of a million every four minutes in great 'muster parades'. They are identical in nearly every respect. The Doctor says they are 'nasty, brutish and short'.

Probic vent – the Sontaran's weak point. Used to absorb energy, but also sensitive to attack

Most Sontarans are short and stocky in stature (some clone batches yielded taller, thinner Sontarans)

Space armour protects against attack

Universal translator unit and scanner in utility belt

Weapon – can kill, stun or hypnotise

Bifurcated hand (but note some batches of Sontarans have human-like five-fingered hands)

RUTANS

The Rutan Empire has been at war with the Sontarans for millennia. The Rutans are green jelly-like blobs with tendril-like appendages, from the cold, icy planet of Ruta 3. They evolved in the sea before adapting to land and are the sworn enemies of the Sontarans.

The Rutan Scout that attacks Fang Rock (see page 87) has been specially trained in 'new metamorphosis techniques' and assumes the form of the lighthouse keeper. It kills with electrical discharges from its body in order to keep its mission secret. It signals to its mothership using power from the lighthouse generator.

The Doctor encounters Commander Linx, a Sontaran.

THE TIME WARRIOR

A Sontaran, Commander Linx, crash-lands in medieval England. He offers a local robber baron, Irongron, advanced weapons in exchange for shelter and help repairing his spaceship. But Linx needs more sophisticated help, and kidnaps scientists from the twentieth century. The Doctor and journalist Sarah Jane Smith travel back in time to find the scientists, and help Sir Edward of Wessex combat Irongron.

Linx kills Irongron as the Doctor and Sarah sneak into the castle and send the scientists home, but Linx has already completed his repairs and is ready to blast off. As Linx prepares to leave, Sir Edward's archer, Hal, hits him in the probic vent with an arrow, killing him.

Written by
Robert Holmes
Featuring
the Third Doctor,
UNIT and Sarah
First broadcast
15 December 1973 –
5 January 1974
4 episodes

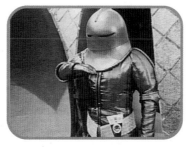

ROBOT KNIGHT

As well as providing breach-loading rifles for Irongron and his men, Linx constructs a robot knight. When Irongron asks if it kills, Linx tells him, 'It does nothing else, and it cannot be killed.'

The knight is operated from a control box, which is damaged when it is shot away with an arrow and the knight goes out of control. Irongron knocks its head off with an axe, and it still 'walks' after falling over. Linx suggests he will make a new knight that will perhaps obey Irongron's voice.

SONTARAN EQUIPMENT

Linx's ship is equipped with an osmic projector (or frequency modulator), which he uses to bring back scientists from the twentieth century. The Doctor says that Linx's spherical scoutship is, like its owner, incredibly powerful for its size.

As well as the translation device on Linx's belt, the Sontaran is armed. He uses his cylindrical gun to knock Irongron's sword away and burn his axe handle. The weapon can also stun or kill, and Linx is able to mesmerise Sir Edward's squire and Sarah so they answer his questions.

STAKING A CLAIM

When Linx arrives on Earth, he claims the planet for the Sontaran Empire. He plants a rod in the ground that opens to reveal the Sontaran flag. Linx then speaks the words of the declaration:

'By virtue of my authority as an officer of the Army Space Corps, I hereby claim this planet, its moons and satellites, for the greater glory of the Sontaran empire...'

Irongron and his followers, watching this curious ritual, are unaware they have just been annexed.

Field Major Styre in full Sontaran battle armour.

THE SONTARAN EXPERIMENT

Written by
Bob Baker and Dave Martin
Featuring
the Fourth Doctor,
Sarah and Harry
First broadcast
22 February 1975 –
1 March 1975
2 episodes

The Doctor, Harry and Sarah arrive on Earth in the far future and find it a barren wasteland, destroyed by solar flares. A group of stranded space travellers from an Earth colony are being observed by Field Major Styre, a Sontaran who is using some of them to assess human strengths. His report is the precursor to a Sontaran invasion of this part of the galaxy.

The Doctor challenges Styre to single combat, and while the Sontaran is distracted Harry sabotages his energy supply. Weakened, Styre tries to re-energise himself, but the energy feeds on him instead and he is killed. The Doctor then persuades the Sontaran Grand Marshal that the humans now know their invasion plans, and the attack is called off.

ABANDONED EARTH

Although it has become strategically important to the Sontarans (in an effort to gain an advantage over the Rutans), Earth has been abandoned by humanity. When it was threatened by solar flares, some humans left to found colonies out in space, while others were selected to go into cryogenic suspension aboard a giant space 'Ark' called Nerva (adapted from Nerva Beacon – see *Revenge of the Cybermen,* page 20). The humans who remained behind went into underground shelters, but perished in the solar flares.

STYRE'S ROBOT

Styre is assisted in his experiment by a robot. Powered by a terulian drive, the robot is resistant to the colonists' weapons, and can shoot out ropes to capture them and hold them immobile. It moves rapidly, even on rough terrain.

The Doctor is able to destroy the robot using his sonic screwdriver.

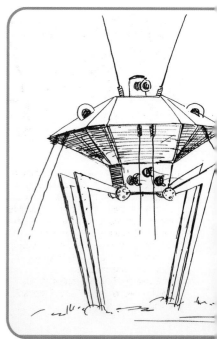

The original Visual Effects design for Styre's frog-like robot.

Commander Stor searches in vain for the Doctor.

THE INVASION OF TIME

The Doctor returns to Gallifrey, but Leela is concerned as he is acting strangely. It seems he has betrayed his people, the Time Lords, to the Vardans – aliens who can travel along any broadcast wavelength. This means that, in effect, they can read thoughts and the Doctor is actually trying to persuade them to materialise fully so he can defeat them.

This done, however, the Doctor discovers that the Sontarans were behind the Vardan invasion – and a battle group of the Sontaran Special Space Service, led by Commander Stor, arrives to take control of Gallifrey. The Doctor lures the Sontarans into the TARDIS, and eventually defeats them using a forbidden demat gun.

Written by
David Agnew
Featuring
the Fourth Doctor,
Leela and K-9
First broadcast
4 February 1978 –
11 March 1978
6 episodes

THE VARDANS

The Vardans can travel along any form of broadcast wavelength and materialise at the end of it – even the TARDIS scanner. They are telepathic, able to read thoughts (even encephalographic patterns), which is why the Doctor has to shield his thoughts. They are humanoid, but until they materialise properly they appear as shimmering silver shapes.

K-9 detects the coordinates of their source planet as vector 3 0 5 2 alpha 7, 14th span.

TIME LORD CEREMONIES

Official Time Lord ceremonies take place in the immense Panopticon on Gallifrey. When the Doctor is invested as President he is 'crowned' with the circlet that gives him access to the Matrix – the repository of all Time Lord knowledge. The ceremony is conducted by Gold Usher, who says, 'It is my duty and privilege, having the consent of the Time Lords of Gallifrey, to invest you as President of the Supreme Council ... I wish you good fortune and strength. I give you the Matrix.'

HORROR OF FANG ROCK

In this adventure broadcast in 1977, the Fourth Doctor and Leela arrive on Fang Rock, a tiny island with only a lighthouse on it. One of the keepers is missing, and another claims that the 'Beast of Fang Rock', which apparently killed the keepers 80 years earlier, has now returned. But this beast is a Rutan scout – surveying Earth for possible use as a base against the Sontarans.

The Doctor manages to destroy the Rutan mothership by converting the lighthouse for use as a giant laser-like beam to shoot the craft down.

Group Marshal Stike is attacked with coronic acid.

THE TWO DOCTORS

Written by
Robert Holmes
Featuring
the Sixth Doctor and Peri,
and the Second Doctor
and Jamie
First broadcast
16 February 1985 –
2 March 1985
3 double-length episodes

The Second Doctor and Jamie investigate time-travel experiments at Space Station Camera. The Sixth Doctor arrives after a Sontaran attack to discover everyone dead, except Jamie. The Doctor realises his earlier self is being held close to Seville by the Sontarans, in league with misguided scientist Dastari, and two Androgums, Shockeye and Chessene.

The Sontarans, under Group Marshal Stike, want to discover the secret of time travel by experimenting on the Doctor. When this fails, Dastari tries to turn the Doctor into an Androgum so he will reveal the secret. Meanwhile, the Sontarans plan to kill Dastari, Shockeye and Chessene – but are themselves tricked and destroyed by Chessene.

ANDROGUMS

The Androgums work as servitors on Space Station Camera, doing all the station maintenance. They are incredibly strong – the Doctor says Shockeye could break both him and Jamie in half with one hand.

Chessene's 'karm name' is Chessene o' the Franzine Grig. Shockeye's karm name is Shockeye o' the Quawncing Grig. He is the station chef and keen to taste human meat after meeting Jamie, so he persuades Chessene to go to Earth.

CLONING SONTARANS

The Sontarans were created by prolific **Doctor Who** writer Robert Holmes. In response to script editor Terrance Dicks's request for a story set in medieval times, Holmes wrote his outline as a citation for Commander Linx, addressed to 'Terran Cedicks' and describing Linx's brave conduct in the events of *The Time Warrior*.

Holmes was reportedly not happy with the notion of writing a pseudo-historical story. He said he was dragged kicking and screaming into it. He boasted that he got his own back later (as script editor) by dragging Terrance Dicks kicking and screaming onto a lighthouse – having him write *Horror of Fang Rock*, which ironically featured the Sontarans' mortal enemy, the Rutans.

THE YETI

The Yeti, or Abominable Snowmen, are creatures that are rumoured to live in the mountainous areas of Tibet, in the Himalayas. But the Yeti encountered by the Doctor and his companions are not the timid creatures of legend. They are fierce robots controlled by an alien intelligence. This Great Intelligence also possessed the Doctor's old friend and master of the Detsen Monastery – Padmasambhava. Through him it controlled the Yeti and planned to take over the world.

With the help of an English explorer, Travers, the Doctor defeated the Intelligence. But this was not to be his last encounter with the Yeti. Forty years later he was to meet them again – in the heart of London.

The Yeti can emit a fierce roar to scare its enemies

Flap covering sphere, through which the Great Intelligence directs the Yeti

Powerful claws – a Yeti can break a rifle in two

The massive Yeti stands over seven feet high

Fur covering to protect the robotic components inside from adverse weather, and possible attack

YETI 'MARK 2'

The Doctor describes the Yeti he meets in present-day London as 'a sort of Mark 2' as they are different from those that he encountered back in 1935 in Tibet.

'Mark 2' Yeti emit a beeping sound when active

Modified feet with shorter claws for urban terrain

Glowing eyes allow Yeti to see in darkened London Underground tunnels

Less bulky Yeti seems even taller

Victoria, Jamie and Travers encounter the Yeti.

THE ABOMINABLE SNOWMEN

Written by
Mervyn Haisman
and Henry Lincoln
Featuring
the Second Doctor,
Jamie and Victoria
First broadcast
30 September 1967 –
4 November 1967
6 episodes

The Doctor visits the Detsen monastery in Tibet in 1935, and discovers it is under threat from the Abominable Snowmen, or Yeti. These shy, timid creatures seem to have become unnaturally aggressive, and the Doctor discovers that they are robots controlled by an alien intelligence that wants to create form and substance for itself on Earth.

But the Doctor realises that this will mean the end of the world, and together with an English explorer, Travers, he manages to destroy the Yeti control centre in the monastery. The Great Intelligence is banished back into a formless existence in space.

CONTROL SPHERE

The Great Intelligence controls the robot Yeti by means of a control sphere – a silver ball that fits inside the Yeti's chest. The Doctor likens the sphere to a brain, and suggests that it is hollow, containing a part of the Intelligence. When outside a Yeti, the sphere can move, rolling along the ground to return to its Yeti and bring it back to life. It emits a beeping sound when it is active. In *The Web of Fear*, the Yeti itself beeps, and the Doctor and his friend Travers adapt a sphere so that it obeys them and not the Intelligence. The Doctor uses it to gain control of a Yeti.

YETI MODELS

Padmasambhava, possessed by the Great Intelligence, uses models of the Yeti positioned on a relief map of the monastery and surrounding area to direct the robots' movements.

In *The Web of Fear*, these models are used by the Intelligence's agent to guide Yeti to their targets – people or places to be destroyed.

PADMASAMBHAVA

The Doctor's old friend, and 'master' of the peaceful Detsen monastery, Padmasambhava is possessed by the Great Intelligence and forced to carry out its orders. He made mental contact with the Intelligence, which has kept him alive for hundreds of years while he built the Yeti robots and other machines to allow the Intelligence to take on a physical form on Earth. When the Intelligence is defeated, Padmasambhava is finally able to die in peace.

A Yeti attacks Anne Travers.

THE WEB OF FEAR

A strange mist has descended over London, which has been evacuated. Yeti roam the deserted streets and the empty tunnels of the London Underground, where a deadly web-like substance is forming.

    The Great Intelligence is back, and the Doctor joins forces with an elderly Travers, his daughter Anne, and an army unit headed by Colonel Lethbridge-Stewart to battle against the Yeti. But the Intelligence has been waiting for the Doctor and intends to drain his mind, using a machine to take his knowledge and experience. The Doctor manages to sabotage the Intelligence's machine and it is again banished from Earth.

Written by
Mervyn Haisman
and Henry Lincoln
Featuring
the Second Doctor,
Jamie and Victoria
First broadcast
3 February 1968 –
9 March 1968
6 episodes

RETURN OF THE YETI

When Travers returned from Tibet after *The Abominable Snowmen*, he brought back 'quite a bit of stuff', including a Yeti, four small Yeti models, and an intact control sphere. He spent many years trying to repair the sphere – until one day he got it working, and the sphere disappeared. Once again controlled by the Intelligence, the sphere sought out the surviving Yeti robot in a private museum. The Yeti returns to life – killing Julius Silverstein, the museum's owner, and giving the Intelligence a bridgehead on Earth.

THE WEB

Also referred to as a 'fungus', the web created by the Intelligence is a mist above ground, and a web below. The Yeti have guns that can fire web at their victims – it kills on contact, smothering them in cobweb-like material. The army has tried chemicals, flame-throwers and even explosives to disperse the web and mist, but without success.

THE ARMY

Headed by Colonel Lethbridge-Stewart following the death of Colonel Pemberton, the army unit battling against the Yeti in London is based in an abandoned transit camp linked to Goodge Street station on the London Underground. In the operations room there is a tube map with lights to show the progress of the fungus–web. With little defence against the Yeti, the army is hoping that Professor Travers and his daughter – later helped by the Doctor – will come up with a scientific solution to the problem of the Yeti and the web.

THE YETI

BRINGING THE YETI TO LIFE

The scripts for *The Abominable Snowmen* and *The Web of Fear* didn't describe the Yeti in any great detail. Costume designer for both these stories was Martin Baugh, who decided on a bear-like creature covered in fur to keep out the cold of Tibet. The costumes for both stories were constructed over a bamboo frame padded with foam rubber for shape and rigidity, and sprayed with black paint to add shade and texture. The result was a huge, impressive creature that viewers could easily believe was capable of smashing aside monks, soldiers and barricades.

Right: A camera crew at the BBC's Ealing film studios captures the sequence when the Yeti attack a soldier in Covent Garden.

Above: This picture shows the image that the director set out to capture – the raw power of the Yeti smashing through a barricade.

Right: The sequence seen from a different angle – as it appeared in Episode 4 of The Web of Fear.

SETTING THE SCENE

Up until the 2005 series, it was usually the case that **Doctor Who** was made mainly in the television studio with some additional work done on location for exterior scenes. To save on the cost of transport and travel, most of the locations used were close to London, but occasionally the production team went further afield.

Although *The Abominable Snowmen* was set in the mountains of Tibet, filming for the story actually took place in the cold and bleak, but less snowy, countryside of the Nant Ffrancon Pass in North Wales. Because it was cold and damp, the ground was slippery and the Yeti often lost their grip and fell over.

For their second encounter with the Doctor, the Yeti attack was focused on London. One of the most exciting sequences was the Yeti attacking soldiers in Covent Garden, which was filmed partly on location in London and partly in the studio.

Although the scenes in the London Underground seemed authentic, they were actually achieved in the television studio. Elements of the set could be repositioned to form different tunnels and sections of station.

The end result was so realistic that London Transport believed the BBC had actually filmed it on their premises without permission, and complained.

Top left: A Yeti actor keeps warm in Wales.

Top right: The impressive set for Piccadilly Circus tube station.

Left: Actor Patrick Troughton (the Doctor) and two Yeti keep out of the rain.

THE ZYGONS

The Zygons are an alien race from a planet destroyed by a stellar explosion. A vast refugee fleet was assembled when the catastrophe struck, but had nowhere to go. However, a group of Zygons led by Broton had been stranded on Earth when their spaceship was damaged. They had been awaiting rescue for centuries. Re-establishing contact with their people, they discovered what had happened and determined to make the Earth their new planet; melting the polar ice caps, raising the overall temperature and creating lakes with a mineral content in which their formidable dinosaur-like Skarasens could thrive.

Broton's spaceship is concealed beneath the waters of Loch Ness, and a Skarasen lives in the loch itself.

Warlord Zygons have enlarged nodules on top of head

Lack of neck gives the Zygon an almost foetal appearance

Hands can interface directly with controls of spaceship built using organic crystallography

ZYGON SHIP

The Zygons on Earth, led by the warlord Broton, arrived in a space-ship that crashed into Loch Ness. It has remained hidden beneath the waters of the loch for centuries.

Built using the Zygons' expertise in organic crystallography, the ship has a dynacron thrust and can emit a radar-jamming signal. A separate chamber provides facilities for body-printing captured humans. There is a self-destruct mechanism operated from the control deck. When the Doctor activates this mechanism, dark fluid rises in three tubes, and when it reaches the top the ship explodes.

Zygons can emit a powerful 'sting' simply by touching their victim

Broton on the control deck of his spaceship hidden in Loch Ness.

TERROR OF THE ZYGONS

The Brigadier calls the Doctor, Sarah and Harry to Scotland to investigate attacks on North Sea oil rigs. The Doctor finds a piece of alien technology – used to guide the creature that attacks the rigs to its target. Sarah is attacked by a 'double' of Harry, which tries to recover the device.

A group of stranded Zygons are using their cyborg Skarasen – which lives in Loch Ness – to attack the rigs. Next they plan to attack an energy conference in London before broadcasting their demands. They want to make the Earth habitable for refugees from their own, destroyed, planet. But the Doctor manages to blow up the Zygon spaceship, and Broton, the Zygon warlord, is killed at the conference.

Written by
Robert Banks Stewart
Featuring
the Fourth Doctor,
Sarah and Harry
First broadcast
30 August 1975 –
20 September 1975
4 episodes

BROTON

Broton, warlord of the Zygons, has assumed the appearance of the Duke of Forgill, the president of the Scottish Energy Commission, which is how Broton is able to enter the conference.

Despite having the appearance of the Duke, Broton is noticeably colder and less sociable. The Duke's servants have left, apart from the Duke's manservant – nicknamed The Caber – who is in fact another disguised Zygon.

Having discovered his planet has been destroyed, Broton determines to turn Earth into a new home for the Zygons.

SKARASEN

The Skarasen is the Zygons' armoured cyborg, dinosaur-like creature living in Loch Ness, often mistaken for the Loch Ness Monster. The Zygons are using it to destroy oil rigs, but this is just a test of strength before Broton destroys more visible targets and makes his demands.

The Skarasen is guided to its target by a target reciprocator. When the Doctor finds one of these devices, Broton activates it, so the creature will attack. The Doctor takes the device to lure the Skarasen away, but the device anchors itself to the Doctor's hand.

BODY PRINTS

The Zygons can take body prints, allowing them to take on the appearance of captive humans. Broton says it is necessary to reactivate a body print every few hours, or else the original pattern will die and cannot be reused. Broton has assumed the identity of the Duke of Forgill (above), while Ola takes the form of Sister Lamont, Madra of Harry, and another Zygon becomes The Caber.